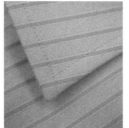

HOW TO SHOP
with Mary,
Queen of Shops

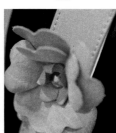

MARY PORTAS

HOW TO SHOP

with MARY, QUEEN OF SHOPS

WITH PETER CROSS, JOSH SIMS
& MELANIE RICKEY

optomen

To Mylo and Verity

This book is published to accompany the television series entitled *Mary, Queen of Shops*, first broadcast on BBC2 in 2007.

10 9 8 7 6 5 4 3 2 1

Published in 2007 by BBC Books, an imprint of Ebury Publishing. A Random House Group Company

The Random House Group Limited Reg. No. 954009

Addresses for companies within the Random House Group can be found at www.randomhouse.co.uk

A CIP catalogue record for this book is available from the British Library.

ISBN 978 1 846 07214 7

The Random House Group Limited makes every effort to ensure that the papers used in our books are made from trees that have been legally sourced from well-managed and credibly certified forests. Our paper procurement policy can be found on www.randomhouse.co.uk

Commissioning editor: Shirley Patton
Project editor: Gillian Haslam
Designer: Smith & Gilmour, London
Photography: Noel Murphy 2007,
except pages 2, 6, 55, Colin Bell 2007; pages 21, 63, 81(tl;br), 118, 153, Andrew Meredith 2007 for Selfridges
Illustrator: Sam Wilson
Printed and bound in Germany by Firmengruppe APPL, aprinta druck, Wemding

optomen

Contents

6 Introduction

10 Shopping in the 21st century

26 Shopping tribes

50 Tricks of the trade

96 When to shop

112 Know before you go

144 Are you being served?

168 Shop stories

182 Directory

191 Index

192 With thanks

Introduction

Shopping is a national pastime. Yet, unlike many of the other ways we spend our time, shopping and shops are not the subject of endless newspaper reviews, makeover shows and 'how to' guides.

We have learnt how to move house in three easy steps, how to decorate a previously unappealing bedroom, how to prepare a lively little curry and how to plant bulbs so they pop up at just the right time. The press tell us which books to read, which movies to see, which restaurants to avoid and which motor cars to buy. We are inundated with ideas on how to dress, get the look, copy the celebrities, even (heaven forbid) dress like an individual. Yet no one is showing us what to look out for once we pass the threshold of the shop itself.

And, let's face it, fashion shopping doesn't come easily to everyone. In fact, quite the opposite is often true. Is it because retailers have such enormous power that no one dared look beyond the mannequins and window sets to see what actually goes on behind the scenes? I think not.

Shopping for clothes, like shopping for food, is one of the things we all have to do, like it or not. Some of us just get on with it and muddle through the process hoping to score more successes than failures. Some of the girls and a larger percentage of the boys hate it, while others are quite frankly too obsessed by it.

When it's at its best, shopping, to me, should be like the best theatre. Fashion shopping should simply be fabulous. There are the clothes themselves: the colours, shapes and textures. There's great service if you're lucky. Window displays should tempt you. The décor, fixtures and fittings, music and mood should transport you to another time or place. Or at least, that is how things ought to be and how it can be, when shops do it well.

Today's shopping world is sadly a very different place. The rise of the mass-market chain store is gradually stripping the personality from our high streets. I have talked with so many friends over the last few years about how dull and uninspiring our high-street shops have become. About how there's no point coming into town because all you get is the same stock in a bigger shop. About how fashion shopping is now so often about commodities and so many of the chains look the same. About how service is shocking. And about how, unless we change things, we'll all end up on the internet and shops will all end up like dull showrooms showcasing what you can buy much more efficiently online.

I write for the Saturday *Telegraph magazine* and visit one shop a week to pass judgement on the store, the service and the overall experience, which I call 'shopability'. I even spend most of my working day in Britain's biggest shops working with our most influential shopkeepers, helping them to pull away from the mundane and dreary and really inspire us.

The reality today, however, is that those people who generally inspire me the most are a handful of brave independents – one-off shops or small groups of stores owned and often managed by the people who founded them – who up the ante and show the big boys what's possible, reminding me why shopping can be fun.

I was crowned 'Mary, Queen of Shops' a few years back by a national newspaper. It's a rather camp title I've earned through working in and with the world's leading luxury and high-street fashion shops, notably Topshop (where I worked 1983–90) and Harvey Nichols (1990–97). I'm not a stylist, I'm not a queen of makeovers. I'm a retail marketing specialist who has a bloody good knowledge of fashion and a passion for making shops positive, fun, stimulating and ultimately satisfying places for the customer. I'm also the founder and creative director of London's best-respected retail marketing agency, Yellowdoor.

My BBC2 television show *Mary, Queen of Shops* takes ailing fashion shops that have lost their way for various reasons. I bring them to Yellowdoor and share with them the tricks we use with the big boys, helping them to sing a more powerful song and hopefully get their lives and their businesses back on track. See pages 168–81 for their stories.

My mission is to make shops better so that you – the customer – get more out of them. This book is my way of letting you in on the secrets of the trade. It's full of the key things I share with my clients (the country's biggest retailers), helping you to get more from your favourite shops and to understand why some shops fail to rock your boat while others give you shopping orgasms! You'll find out how to recognise the shopping tribes (a key tool I use with my clients to identify and target their customers), how to shop better for different products, how shops work from the outside in, how to recognise the worst culprits in our often dismal service culture and how to complain if things go wrong.

But this book is not for the businessperson or store manager, though they sure could learn a few things by dipping into it over their tea-break. Nor is it a book that claims shopping to be the be-all and end-all of life. Rather, this is a book for you, the shopper. It is not simply a reminder of how great shopping can be but also a look at how you can get the best out of the best shops – I shall take you behind the scenes, through that door marked 'staff only', to show you the tricks of the trade, to show you not only how to shop efficiently, quickly and with good value, but also how to get more out of those shops you'd never even imagined entering.

Napoleon said that the British were a nation of shopkeepers. What he overlooked was that we are also a nation of shoppers. If he had invaded England on a Saturday afternoon we might not even have noticed.

It's almost 9am. That's opening time. Let's go shopping!

Mary Portas

SHOPPING IN THE 21st CENTURY

And God said, 'Let there be shopping'. OK, so it wasn't quite that simple, but rudimentary shops of a kind that would be recognisable to modern consumers have been part of culture since each substituted money (in the guise of coins and, later, notes) for the original bartering system of exchange – I give you one candle, you give me two loaves. Just think eBay.

Indeed, some theories argue that it was shops that gave rise to cities, in as much as overland trading routes, such as the Silk and Spice Routes linking Asia with Europe, covered such vast distances that centres in which merchants could rest and, over time, base themselves and trade became established along them.

But jump forward millennia and shops have become the new cities. The fastest-growing format for shops today – both in terms of numbers and size – is the mall: huge, convenient, comprehensive and, for many people, soulless. So, what's the answer? How can we reinvent the shopping trip as an event to look forward to? The first step is to understand what we shoppers are looking for from our 21-st century shops.

Value

Value retailers have changed the way we shop. If we used to buy investment designer pieces, shunning the high street's cheapo copies as much as possible, now there has been a sea change in attitude. The kudos now lies not just in snagging a designer must-have, but also in how good a bargain you can get. This is the era of the £20 outfit, and the so-called 'bargainista' shopper.

This isn't all good news for the shops mind: because we're getting more for our money (or so it seems at least), our spend per head each year is not actually going up much: just £12 at the last count, and all but 20p of that went to value retailers – TK Maxx, Matalan, New Look, the supermarket clothing ranges such as those from Asda and Tesco, and of course Peacocks and Primark or, as the fashion insiders have come to call it, 'Primani'.

That's putting a squeeze on the money that these shops can make, forcing other brands to lower their prices to compete – such that the middle market has become a bit of a desert – and has even thrown the designer labels into confusion. If you, the shopper, are happy to mix designer with high street (and you are, such that value clothing now accounts for a quarter of the entire market), then how does their traditional plan of selling to the elite stand up these days? It doesn't.

The question is: how long can this last? Firstly, the only way to stay alive as a retailer with these prices is to sell a lot – and I mean a lot – of clothes. And unless you're going to build a short shelf-life into the clothes – either through making very trend-aware pieces, or those that just don't last long before falling apart – that's getting harder all the time. Secondly, the ethical shopper is starting to ask awkward question: why is this dress only £4? Who's suffering where to make it possible to sell at that price? And, thirdly, there are rumours that the middle market is bouncing back – we're tired of cheap tat and want longer-lasting quality. That's the theory anyway. Watch your high street and follow your shopping nose – what happens next is down to the way you shop.

Ethical clothing

Once the only questions that came with fashion shopping were 'Do I like it?', 'Do I look good in it?' and, sometimes, 'Can I afford it?' Now we add to that 'Where was it made, who made it and from what?' and 'How come it's so cheap?'. Clothing, in other words, has become an ethical issue. We've had the anti-sweatshop movement for some years and many companies have responded positively – not only in the spirit of 'corporate responsibility' but also, if you ask me, in the spirit of protecting long-term profits. We're looking at websites and listening to the organisations that investigate these issues and taking their recommendations as to which brands are taking the right steps. Pioneers in this field include Patagonia, American Apparel and Katharine Hamnett, and specialist labels like People Tree and Ali Hewson's (a.k.a. Mrs Bono) label Edun.

But now we've gone organic in our food, we're also going organic in our fabrics, cotton especially. The world's biggest non-food crop is also the biggest user of insecticides and pesticides (nearly 25 per cent of the world's use of these chemicals) and Big Business wants to keep it that way, even though it poisons water courses at a time when clean water is more precious than oil and, in many instances, the farm workers who handle the crops, resulting in thousands of deaths every year. Cotton growing has even created environmental disasters in some parts of the world. So much for cotton being the pure, natural stuff they sniff in the washing-powder ads...

The organic cotton market in the UK has grown by 50 per cent a year recently, with high-street retailers (including Tesco, who are working with Katharine Hamnett, and Marks & Spencer) starting to offer organic cotton ranges, even though difficulties in growing organic cotton make supply unpredictable and thus hard to use for fast fashion. Shoppers like you and I should support them by asking for organic cotton and buying it whenever there is the option.

The internet

Why schlepp through the rain and crowds to buy fashion when you can do so with your backside making a dent in your cosy armchair? It's a no-brainer, right? Wrong. Shopping online for clothes didn't take off immediately. Part of the pleasure of shopping – out in the real world, that is – is seeing so many options, being able touch them all, see them up close and try them on before you buy (not forgetting shopping's pleasure in making a fun day out of it). There's also the instant gratification of seeing it and buying it there and then. Yes, you can wait for your internet purchase to turn up in a few days and then return it if it's not suitable, but it's a hassle. Perhaps this is why only 3 per cent of clothing sales are from the internet and why the leading players are companies that have successfully traded through catalogues for years anyway.

Then again, retail analysts predict that the internet will be one of the fastest-growing markets for fashion shopping in the years to come, with the market increasing by over 130 per cent in the next four years, they reckon. It has its advantages of course: it is a great place to track down rare, discontinued, vintage or other 'hard to get' items; and eBay and other auction sites can sometimes let you get it at a great price, although I always manage to end up in some desperate bidding war. In 2006 sales of fashion over the internet in the UK topped the £1bn mark for the first time – that's a whopping 461 per cent increase over the past five years, as more retailers have launched online sales and more people taken up broadband. Perhaps, inevitably, it's the younger shopper, aged 15–24 who is most likely to buy fashion online. Who said teenagers were lazy?

Think it's only men who are techie? Women use the internet to buy clothing more than men: 42 per cent compared with 34 per cent. But then women also buy more groceries online than men too. Some things never change.

Vintage

Vintage fashion has become a bona-fide phenomenon in the last decade. If you wanted to demonstrate individuality, dressing vintage was cool. Maybe it's a reflection of just how homogenised so much high-street fashion is these days that we now look to the past. Maybe it's because the quality was better. Maybe we're just hungry for something unique in a world of mass-manufacturing – an item you know you won't see 20 other people wearing as you walk to the bus-stop (just how annoying is that?). Some think that vintage is a rip-off: some old tat given an inflated price tag just because it's old (which doesn't automatically make it desirable). Others think it's a source of 'inspiration' – fashion designers have been known to rip off vintage clothing for their own collections.

Certainly the market has its share of shysters: vintage is a term much abused and increasingly applied to last year's collections, rather than items that genuinely embody a sense of an era or a key place in fashion's evolution. It's a great bit of spin: unwanted 80s and 90s clothes that would have found a home in a charity shop just a few years ago are now reborn as covetable and deserving of worship (these are really 'contemporary' or maybe 'retro' and not true 'vintage' – think anything from the 1920s to 1960s for that). It seems that any Hollywood starlet only has to wear a bit of 'vintage' on a red carpet to be re-appraised as a style icon these days.

But the market for vintage is undoubtedly booming and if nothing else it's good for the environment that so much recycling is going on and charity shops now have a case for putting up prices. Specialist shops and internet auction sites and retailers have opened up, high-street stores have created 'vintage' concessions – sat alongside their 'vintage look' new stock – while the famed flea markets of Paris and London (Camden and Portobello especially) have been reborn as fashion meccas (always check condition, sizing and, with expensive items, authenticity). There's nothing new in this – until the 1950s people regularly bought second-hand clothes, maybe remodelling them at home. That's fashion: what goes around, comes around.

London now

OK, so the fashion world in the UK does not revolve around London. Anyone with some sense will know that shopping in, say, Manchester or Leeds is far less painful than struggling through the tourist masses in the capital to get to that one sparkly top you can see glinting in the distance but can't quite reach. That said, London is becoming a global shopping destination that genuinely rivals the other 'fashion capitals' of New York, Paris and Milan. Foreigners especially tend to equate fashion shopping in London with the King's Road – birthplace of punk, epicentre of the so-called Swinging Sixties – which has been lifted thanks to redevelopment at the Sloane Street end, though much of its famed boutique character has been replaced by stores turning it into yet another high street.

But there's much more going on in London too: Notting Hill has seen a whole host of new boutiques springing up, making the area a hotspot (especially on Fridays and Saturdays when Portobello Market is on). Bond Street (which technically doesn't exist – there's Old Bond Street which runs into New Bond Street, giving plenty of room to have fun with lost tourists here) has been an upmarket destination since the 18th century and today is a must for (rich) watch and jewellery fans especially. Its environs are also getting funkier, with big designer brands choosing its side streets to open major flagship stores, picking up a bit of Bond Street cachet without paying Bond Street rents. The whole area has undergone something of an overhaul. Nearby Savile Row has been home to the world's finest men's tailoring since 1785. Not only has it been turned around by an influx of both new tailors and new thinking, but it is now a draw to major fashion brands that want to be situated near by.

Even Oxford Street isn't the dire spot it once was. It still takes balls to shop there – the crowds can be overwhelming (they used to hang criminals at the western end of the street – they should have sent them shopping). But a street that encompasses Selfridges, the world's largest Marks & Spencer, Watches of Switzerland, Nike Town and a gigantic Primark all on the same stretch has to be a winner.

The high street

People who read the tea leaves are always saying that the high street is dead, and it's certainly true that with the growth of out-of-town retail parks during the 80s and 90s it looked as though they may have been right. But the high street seems busier than ever. Britain's fashion strength is in the high street – fashion for all. And great fashion at that. We rule the world market for well-priced, well-designed clothes.

The big high-street brands are having to be very clever about it because although millions of pounds of profit are being made, the competition is stiff and positions in the league table are constantly shifting. Although Marks & Spencer has had troubled times, it has reinvented itself and is still the market leader, but at the last count, in 2007, that still only accounts for 12 per cent of the womenswear market in the UK. Arcadia has just over 9 per cent and Next about 7 per cent. And all the other key players, from the Mosaic Group (which owns Oasis and Karen Millen) to Primark, New Look and Debenhams, all have around 3 per cent. In other words, there's not much between them. They're all desperate for your cash.

That's why they're keen to create a buzz and reassert their authority by, for instance, signing established designer names and even the odd celebrity or fashion model to create special collections. They're coming up with business plans that include consolidation (getting different brands under one umbrella and benefiting from their combined strength), launching new concepts (often into more upmarket or niche parts of the fashion territory) or extending their brands in new directions. 'We sell clothes. Hey, why don't we sell homewares too!' It's not original but it seems to get us 'lifestyle consumers' in the mood again. In other words, the high street is a dynamic and ever-changing theatre of business and shopping. Keep your eyes peeled and your mitts tight around that purse.

The malls

Going to a mall always made me feel I was stepping into a twilight zone where there was no sense of whether it was day or night, or what the weather was doing outside. I hate that. That was the idea, of course. Cut off from real life, you forget how much money you're spending. Most of them were like maximum-security prisons with shops – and always the same damn shops. Add to this the fact that they are often built over the top of lovely old shops, or end up closing those shops as they drag local customers away, and you might say I'm not their number-one fan. It doesn't surprise me that in the US shootings always seem to happen in malls. They are that depressing.

That said, they are getting better. It has taken them 30 years to do so, ever since Brent Cross became the UK's first indoor shopping centre in 1976, but better late than never. This has largely been due to extensive refurbishment (such as Brent Cross underwent a decade ago and the £500,000 recently spent just on the loos!). But it has also been because many, such as Bluewater, have pulled in a more interesting selection of stores and others, like Bicester Village, have gone for a more welcoming, less oppressive format altogether, just like, well, a village. New developments, such as London's Westfield, which opens in 2008, are also attempting something more human: with an undulating glass roof, it is set to be an intriguing building. And one that won't just cover some 270 (count 'em!) shops, but an indoor atrium for arts and fashion events.

In other words, although malls have long been gathering places – for the hoodies, at least – there are attempts to make them more appealing, to make them a good experience, to give shoppers more reason to pay them a visit other than the dull fact that 'everything is under one roof'. Although the pace of development is slowing, malls are still being built, especially in out-of-town locations, because 'destination' retailing has become the key thinking (even chains are building fewer, bigger stores now). With the competition rising, that means they're going to have to get much better. That's good news for you and me.

Big-city slickers

It's easy, when you live there, to think that London is the be-all and end-all of fashion shopping in the UK. But it only takes a couple of hours on a train to realise how wrong this is. The bigwigs who run London's famed department stores (most notably Selfridges and Harvey Nichols) have realised this too. In recent years they have started setting up shop in many of the UK's major metropolitan centres. In part this is because, although the nation's wealth is still weighted towards the Southeast, it is spreading further afield, while the stereotypes – ideas that it's 'grim up north', or that Birmingham, for instance, is more roundabout than city – are being disproven by experience.

Among recent developments, Birmingham's Bullring, for example, now has 140 shops and £500,000 is spent there every day (and not all by me). Manchester has its Tib Street fashion market and its Northern Quarter. Leeds has seen redevelopment of its Corn Exchange, Kirkgate Market and Victoria Quarter, together with The Light, a city-centre shopping complex. Without a long history of dominance by the major high-street chains, it is in the regional capitals where the best independents are often found too.

Indeed, glossy shopping facilities are springing up all over the country, with a vast amount of money flowing into the regions, centred around key major cities: those mentioned above, and with the likes of Liverpool, Newcastle, Glasgow, Bristol, Middlesbrough and Cardiff also seeing major advances. Aspirations – as well as property prices and rents – are rising everywhere. A lot of it may be founded on easy credit, but there is a nationwide demand for a higher standard of living, and for many that entails spending their disposable income on being better dressed.

The fashion independents

It's really to the fashion independents up and down the UK that this book, and the accompanying television series, is dedicated. They face an uphill battle with rents (some rising as much as 400 per cent over the last decade), struggle to find spots that get some passing trade, have to compete with giant brand names with giant shops and giant marketing budgets, but in my opinion the best shopping is always to be found at an independent

It's true that their less-than-central location may mean you have to go out of your way to visit them, but the fact is that their selection has been carefully chosen for a particular type of shopper – you. It's a selection often sourced from the kind of unexpected, little-known manufacturers (i.e. not the powerfully promoted mega-brands) that you simply won't find anywhere else and they are all unfailingly inspiring. If you want to dress like you, find out who 'you' is and shop at the independents.

Finding the treasures independents offer up is what makes shopping with them much more exciting than going to a high-street store – somehow with those you always have a pretty accurate idea of what you'll find inside before you've even stepped over the threshold. Find the right independents for you and you'll also find your loyalty to them growing because they will save you so much time. Suddenly there's no need to go trailing around shop after shop: just a few have your taste nailed and all your needs catered to. They also tend to have a small, well-trained staff who know their onions and are keen to have your best interests at heart. And the staff will make sure they know you – a phone call when the stock you like arrives is like manna from heaven. Unsurprisingly, you can't say that about the Saturday boys and girls who tidy the rails of most high-street stores.

I'm not above begging, but consider this a personal plea to support the independent shops in your area, and those you find on your travels. It's these shops that give the flavour to our streets and, I feel, do the most to make shopping for fashion what it should be: fun.

SHOPPING TRIBES

Forget star signs – there's no better way to determine someone's personality and character than by working out to which of my shopping tribes they belong .

If an anthropologist took a good look at the British high street, they would see that it was not thronging with just one species of clothes shopper. Rather, there are many, overlapping for sure, but definitive enough to set one apart from another. Knowing tribes helps retailers and their market-research consultants better to define their customers, allowing them to buy the right stock and set the right tone in their stores accordingly.

What's your tribe?

Each type dresses and shops in a specific way, both in terms of the brands they seek out, the look they like and their motivation for favouring it. You may well spot your friends among these types. Go on – have a chuckle at their expense. Of course, you won't (unless you're honest) spot yourself. Nobody likes to be a 'type'. But I bet you're in here.

The Classicist

You have to be tough to be a Classicist. It's a bit like saying you like Beethoven in the middle of a Westlife gig – you're liable to be considered a bit fuddy-duddy, a bit behind the times, a bit old before your time. But the Classicist knows differently of course, especially when it comes to going the distance. For that pink puffball skirt her friend paid a few hundred for in that swanky department store – 'Pink is so in, volume is so in!' she exclaimed – will be gathering dust, shunned even by moths, at the bottom of the wardrobe in a matter of months. The Classicist, meanwhile, can chuckle to herself: she is still wearing clothes she bought years ago, and will still be wearing the clothes she buys today in years to come. And she looks good too.

She may not look all that exciting, mind. Nobody is going to mark her down as a fashion pin-up. Trends, frankly, come and go while she repeats her own mantra: simple shapes, the best natural fabrics, detail over ostentation, a neutral palette and lots and lots of navy. The result may age her a little. It may give her a rather serious air. She may sometimes be mistaken for a Revenue & Customs official or the hotel manager.

But the way she dresses exudes timeless quality. None of the great style icons was a fashion bunny, she will tell you. That's why we're still copying their style – because it was essentially classicist and hasn't dated. What is more, though she may spend more on a single item than others do on their entire new-season wardrobe, somehow she still gets better value. Now that may not light fireworks, but that is clever shopping.

Shops at: Nicole Farhi, Maxmara, Joseph, Tods, Hermes, John Smedley, Chanel, Paul Smith, Margaret Howell.

She's past suffering for fashion. She knows what she wants and she's past caring if it's cool. Sod that!

The Forever Forty

The Forever Forty is the most powerful woman in fashion because she has the most money and the experience to know what's what. Fashion has for ever been associated with youth – witness the furore over the fashion magazines the minute one of them 'dares' to use a model over 40 – but it is, in fact, the 'lady of a certain age' (i.e. over 50) who calls the shots. She used to be called 'The Grey Pounder', but she's no longer grey as she colours her hair and she has more than a pound to spend, believe you me. She's loaded and in charge.

I call her my 'forever forty' woman. She might be in her fifties or sixties, but in her head she has stayed at the age when she felt at her most powerful and at her most beautiful – and that is forty-ish.

Thanks to better healthcare and lower birth rates, the average national age is getting older. Thanks to the fact that retired people can have a higher disposable income – hence the term 'grey pound', though they're not necessarily grey and not necessarily doing much pounding anymore either – and a readiness to spend it on more than a blue rinse and set, fashion companies are waking up to her and giving her great clothes. And thanks to powerplate fitness machines, plastic surgery and elasticised waistbands, she is able to wear them beautifully.

That's not because the Forever Forty is fat, but because her over-riding concern is comfort as well as style. She's been blistered for her high heels, she's wiggled in pencil skirts and minis, burned her bra, strutted her power suit and wafted in a kaftan. Now she wants it all without the pain.

The point being that she's past suffering for fashion. Hence the sight of the Grey Pounder trawling the rails of Debenhams or John Lewis for safe, loose-fitting trousers (so much more convenient than skirts), feminine blouses they can wear loose and untucked and scarves with which to hide the wrinkly neck. This simply means she knows what she wants, and she's past caring if it's cool. Sod that!

But whatever you do, do not underestimate the Forever Forty. She is not to be limited by outdated ideas of 'dressing her age'.

Diana Lazarris's shop in Banstead (see page 175) was perfectly placed to target this tribe. Although far from seeing them as forever forty, dear Diana had them all dressed in hospital dressing gowns, just about ready to head off through the pearly gates. Instead, she wanted Nicole Farhi and Seven for All Mankind jeans.

The Forever Forty can, of course, be male too. But while some are stuck with the quaint if charming sartorial rules they adhered to 30 years ago (no man should be seen in public without a collar and tie, for instance, while a hat is not something to keep your head warm, but a device for tipping to 'ladies of a certain age'), generally it seems that the older a man gets, the less interested he is in clothes. This is no doubt a consequence of one too many Christmases when he was given yet another pair of checked slippers. Give him distressed denim next time.

Shops at: John Lewis, Hobbs, Jaeger, Wallis, Debenhams, Principles, Gap, Basler, Jacques Vert, Viyella, Country Casuals, Planet.

The Fashionista

The Fashionista is no mere lazy Label Lover. In fact, the labels she loves are likely to leave you mere mortals dumbfounded – you may hear of them in a year or so's time if you keep your ear to the ground. By then they will be old hat to her. Speaking of old hats, she may well wear one – something extravagant, as though she were going to a posh wedding but got lost on the way. She, after all, is the one at the cutting edge of the cutting edge.

Being so gives her licence to dress in a certain way: she is the avant garde embodied in cotton, wool and lots of funny experimental fabrics. She thinks like Henry Ford – you can have any colour as long as it's black. Japanese designers – especially the conceptual ones, those prone to making jackets with three sleeves – are her gods. Although her Japanese is limited to 'Wonderful darling' and 'How much?', some are even her close friends. So she says. This is why she always seems to refer to designers by their first names. To you, he's Mr Armani. To her, he's Giorgio. They have never met.

Being so dedicated to the artistry of the designer also allows her certain foibles: she likes to spout technical jargon and refers to individual garments not as 'clothes' but as 'pieces', as though they stood in a gallery with a 'do not touch' sign. That, in fact, is what fashion is to her: it's not fun, it's art. Shopping is an intellectual exercise. Don't even think of asking her if your bum looks big in this.

Shops at: London's Dover Street Market, Superbrand section of Selfridges, Martin Margiela, Comme des Garçons, Helmut Lang, Issey Miyake.

Action Man

While most of us think of wellies and tents as being the opposite of fashion (unless they're at a cool music festival), Action Man embraces the outdoorsy way of life, from the mindset to the way he wears it. If fashion takes on a more masculine bent, he will be at its extreme: where fashion sees sturdy boots, he sees hiking boots; where fashion sees combat trousers, he sees multi-pocketed, waterproof, nylon-polyester blend trousers in various shades of moss that he can openly call 'action pants' with absolutely no sense of irony. Even if fashion doesn't see it, he sees it. He is outside fashion.

Ask him about the labels he is wearing and he won't tell you that his 'moisture-wicking' T-shirt is from North Face or Patagonia, or his pac-a-mac from Rohan or Helly Hansen. He's more interested in the label's small print. He'll tell you that his grey zip-up fleece is shower-resistant and windproof with a shell made from 97 per cent bullet-proof Kevlar (or some such hi-tech fabric), and 3 per cent elastane, for added comfort, 'because you need to be able to stretch when you're halfway up a mountain'.

The fact is that the highest he goes is the top level of the multi-storey carpark. Action Man likes the romance of adventure, but is rarely active himself, though he did go to the Lake District once (stayed in a B&B, a 'hike' to the pub each day, got high on Kendal Mint Cake). He would rather mooch around Millets or Blacks than actually get too far away from the comforts of home. Instead, what really excites him is the functionality of the clothing. It doesn't aim to look good. It aims to do only what it says on the tin. It works, especially in the urban jungle of middle England – and it makes him look like Action Man. And that's all that matters.

Shops at: Blacks, Gant, Millets, Timberland, CAT, Levi's, North Face, Patagonia, Rohan, Helly Hansen.

Miss Vintage

Fashion is all about reinvention and recycling, and nobody knows this better than Miss Vintage. She's even recycled the language. After all, before it became trendy, 'vintage' – for all its connotations of the classic, of class and of fine wines – was better known as 'second hand'. And, at worst, it was known as smelly charity-shop tat which, although funding a worthwhile cause, was often musty with mothballs and stained with suspicious marks. Back then only serious collectors touched it. These days, as Miss Vintage might point out, it's a step above the most chichi of designer clothing.

Why? Not only because sometimes it is designer clothing, but it's designer clothing that not any old bruiser with a big bank account can get. Vintage implies rarity, and in a world of international mass-market fashions, in which even designerwear is copied and on the high street before the designerwear, that is worth paying for.

And this Miss Vintage does: vintage clothes that just a few years ago Oxfam couldn't give away free with an old Stephen King paperback and a Max Bygraves' tape (ask your mum) can now sometimes sell for thousands. If once vintage were suspect (there's a reason it's old and still pristine: nobody wore it), now vintage equals prestige.

Of course, there is vintage that is really retro – those hideous polyester shirts, kipper ties and anything else that should have been put down in the 1970s

'Vintage' to her is just another kind of must-have brand. When the backlash comes, she'll be the first to say that new is the new new.

but, thanks to all that manmade fibre, have, like nuclear waste, lived on beyond their time.

There's vintage which is designerwear from the 1980s onwards given marketing spin – the kind of stuff some people still have in their wardrobes, which only appeals to shoppers who can't really remember the 80s the first time around.

And then there is vintage proper – clothing from a pre-brand era that requires a grasp of fashion history really to appreciate and a degree of patience to find, not to mention a taste for supreme workmanship and the fetish for utter beauty of fashion expression. Going through the rails of Rellik on London's Golborne Road is, to me, really vintage shopping – a true joy.

Funnily enough, this variety is largely lost on Miss Vintage. If she were clever she'd see vintage as a way of by-passing the whole fashion system of rehashing the past by going direct to source, even if that means repeated dry-cleaning to remove that musty smell that seems to inhabit all vintage-clothing stores. Sadly, 'vintage' to her is just another kind of must-have brand. When the backlash comes, she'll be the first to say that new is the new new. And the word 'oxymoron' will be totally lost on her.

Shops at: Top Shop vintage section, Oasis new vintage, Oxfam Origin, markets and second-hand shops nationwide.

The Bag Hag

Call it an obsession, given how many of these receptacles they can have in the wardrobe. Call it irresponsible, especially given the amount of money some of them cost. But the Bag Hag's desire for beautifully designed leathergoods small and large knows no bounds. Never mind clothes – they're a side issue. Somewhere, sometime, the Bag Hag read that the fastest way to update a tired look is with a new handbag. And she took that advice to heart.

Unfortunately her way is not typically born of a talent for throwing on an old necklace discovered at a flea market, or a belt borrowed from her mum, and making the old look fantastically stylish again. No, this is more about one-upmanship. There are a few women, of course, who simply lust after bags in the way some – no, I mean all – women lust after shoes. Because they're sculptural. Because they're snazzy. Because they're useful. Just because, OK?

But with clutches, sacks and cases, more often it's just a case of preparing for handbags at dawn: a fashion duel in which no blood is spilled, in which perhaps nothing is even said, but in which one woman knows that her bag is cooler/rarer/more expensive than that of her opponent (better known as her friend and colleague).

Rather like a man and the right watch, the bag is a shortcut to a certain kind of fashion credibility: you don't have to have a certain body shape to wear it and it doesn't have to complement your skin tone. You just have to have the money and the determination to be first in line – the cash and the dash – to get it before it sells out. It's a points thing.

What's even better is that showing it off requires no effort at all and looks perfectly innocent. You just have to fill it with the usual random selection of cosmetics, old biros, scraps of paper with nameless phone numbers, kitchen sink, and hold it.

But when I say the bag, I mean the bag. At any one moment – and often just for a moment – there is always just one bag that is the It-bag, the bag that was created to have that meaningless phrase 'must have' applied to it. 'Must have' or what, exactly? But as far as the Bag Hag is concerned, must-have it is. (Note to men in the life of the Bag Hag – don't even try to understand why she needs dozens of bags, or why this bag is any more special than the last one. You will never get it.)

Shops at: Harvey Nichols, Selfridges, London's Bond Street and Sloane Street, or wherever there is a label and a logo.

The Nerd

The Nerd is typically in his 20s – or in his 30s and wishing he was in his 20s. Either way, because of his absolute devotion to T-shirts, jeans and beaten-up trainers, he looks young-ish, if not positively teen-like given his scruffy ways. If he had a bedroom you'd want to send him there to tidy it up. But one shouldn't scoff. For while the Nerd may look as though fashion were the last thing on his mind – and Britney Spears the first – he is actually obsessive about his clothing. Perhaps not the way it looks exactly, but its provenance.

Duffer, Y2K, A Bathing Ape, Carhartt are his watchwords. For his is, for example, not just a bog-standard T-shirt. It is a limited-edition piece bearing a design by some obscure Norwegian street artist of whom you have almost certainly never heard (neither had he before he Googled them). The graphic will either involve some cutesy animal figure, a witty reworking of a famous corporate logo or a phrase that sounds insightful, political or philosophical, but that on closer consideration is mostly meaningless.

The jeans, meanwhile, will be Japanese reproductions of an original 1950s style made on hand looms abandoned by Levi's in the 1890s. They will probably have a selvage – the little blue and red stripe that runs along the inner seam of the leg – that he may show off by wearing a turn-up. And they will definitely be baggy in the arse department.

You'll know this because most of the time you'll be able to see his greying Calvins, so low are his jeans worn. And as for his trainers, no, they're not old. Well, they are, but they are old in the new way: they're original Nike Air Jordan 13s or some such, acquired on eBay for a week's wages.

The point of all this precision-shopping? It makes him feel fashion elite in an unglitzy way. It creates a code that only those of a similar sensibility will appreciate. And it generates its own in-crowd.

Shops at: independent fashion boutiques nationwide, Size? for trainers and Clarks originals.

Dapper David

Dapper David thinks he's really cool. And always neat and tidy. He squints rather than smiles – to do so would crumple his face, and nothing on Dapper David is crumpled. The placement of every crease has been considered. His hair is short and neatly cut, and he holds his cappuccino (double shot, no foam, extra hot) as though he's trapped in a French art-house movie. In fact, there is something very Euro about Dapper David: his look is the kind pursued by wealthy French and Italians who favour a stylised idea of how the English gentry dress, and by British gents who have an idea of how French and Italians dress while imitating the English. This is to say a crisp open-neck shirt, always with cufflinks, single-breasted jacket, a pair of nice jeans and a pair of dressy brogues or slip-on suede loafers.

We used to call him the metrosexual, but I found that a bit silly. Either you're Arthur or Martha. And he's quite happy being David.

None of his clothes is overtly branded (though he does have a penchant for Hugo Boss and Zegna), but all of it will be of the utmost quality.

Shops at: Massimo Dutti when he can't afford to go to Europe, Hugo Boss, Thomas Pink, Zegna, and a little Reiss and Zara now and again.

CHELSEA BRIDGE
ROAD. S.W.1.

The Posh Girl

Posh Girl's dress sense is, like the money with which she goes shopping, mostly inherited. To the upper classes, or those who aspire to them, fashion is something of a dirty word. One goes to one's dressmaker or where mummy shops – they have been a provisioner of the finest ladieswear to her family for generations. In other words, it's less about this season's trends and more about a certain style. Her mother's.

Look at a Posh Girl from a distance and it is hard to place her age any more accurately than somewhere between 30 and 60. What is certain is that she dresses older than she is: traditionally, like an off-duty 'something in the city' – which she may well be – or a girl in PR. To speak of duty here is, of course, rather appropriate. With her family's military background stamped on some part of the family tree, it is perhaps inevitable that Posh Girl likes a bit of a uniform.

The shoes are little heels or loafers. The trousers, for posh ladette likes her trousers, are narrow, or jeans, always stonewashed, perhaps artfully distressed, never a consequence of prolonged wear. The blouse is prim, worn with a brooch. Alternatively, it is a polo shirt – Ralph Lauren, Crew or Hackett preferably – with the collar worn turned up, as though fresh from the final chukka.

Actual professional polo shirts, of the kind by the likes of La Martina, may also be worn, for much the same reasons as the terrace oikette wears a football shirt – to show allegiance, to bask in reflected athleticism. Over the shirt is found her boyfriend's sweater – rarely actually worn, but carried around the shoulders like a pashmina of which she is also fond. A hairband keeps her long, straight, feminine-if-unfancy hair out of her eyes.

Nothing fancy is what she's all about really. The fabrics she wears may be more from the huntin', fishin' and shootin' school of style – tweeds, suede, lots of moleskin and waxed cotton – but the way they are put together signals from one Posh Girl to another that she is safely consorting with old money and none of that nouveau stuff. The lower classes may sometimes ape her style and choice of brands. But if in doubt, check her shoes. If she's wearing white Reeboks, her estate is more the council than the 100-acre variety.

Shops at: Crew Clothing Co., Ralph Lauren, Gap, Tods, Hackett, Jack Wilson, Boden.

The Bargainista

Time was when the Bargainista was a fashion outsider. Designerwear meant big bucks – that was what gave it its exclusivity, what kept the badly dressed masses in their place. So anyone who shopped in sub-high-street stores or only set foot inside a brand-name shop during sale time – and then right at the end of the sale, after the final mark-downs – was considered a bit of a loser, at least in fashion terms.

But, things have changed. These days not only is designer fashion a mass-market affair with all those diffusion lines making the brands accessible to almost everyone, but it is also a high-street affair with all those designers revamping their credibility by creating limited-edition lines for high-street brands. If once boasting about how much a fashion item cost was the done thing (vulgar, I know), now, in the eBay age, boasting about what a bargain you got has become, as they say in France, de rigueur.

Suddenly, the Bargainista seems like the hippest chick around. She's the one who loves her fashion but, either because she's money-minded or a bit short at the moment, can find the look of Prada in Primark or Armani in Matalan.

Suddenly, she doesn't look poor or tight but very smart, and certainly no victim of designer hype and its super-boosted prices. There may have been times when she might have liked to have splashed out on Bond Street. But these days it's the splashers who are trying to work out how she does it.

Because being the Bargainista takes skill. It needs an ability to distil the essence of each season's trends and recapture that in items bought for a few quid in stores your average fashionista would not even admit having heard of. And it needs a stylist's skill to pull them all together well. So here's the bitter pill for some to swallow: the bargain queen often looks better dressed than the designer diva.

Shops at: factory outlets, eBay, Primark, Matalan, TK Maxx, Tesco's Florence and Fred, George at Asda.

The Saturday Nighter

The aristocracy of revolutionary France referred to the masses as the Great Unwashed. Skip forward 300 years and across the Channel and we might refer to the Great Untucked. This is the characteristic look of the Saturday Nighter: high-street loafers, a pair of Farah slacks and, of course, the shirt, probably a Ben Sherman button-down or a YSL, left flailing in the wind. Critically, it's all about choosing and wearing the right brands. To get this wrong is social suicide. A baseball cap may be squeezed over the copious amounts of wet-look gel, and a chunky necklace worn over the collar finishes it off. The women are no better: bared midriff, blue legs, pastels and neon shades, everything too tight or too short for modesty – or, for that matter, their figures – and copious amounts of make-up (well, at least their faces will be warm).

Perhaps the only other essential item is the one they wear wherever they go: a cloud of fragrance that evacuates lifts and sets off smoke detectors.

This is not to say the Saturday Nighter has not made an effort – or at least an effort to blend in with his mates or girlfriends. If, for many, fashion is about personal expression, for the Saturday Nighter it's about clan membership and peer approval. To deviate from what his group considers acceptable would be to invite ridicule.

But, in a way, they have at least made the effort – their weekend kit includes track pants and the much villified hoodie. Now, as any grown man knows, anything with a hood is to be avoided at all costs. Hoods are for toddlers and Mancunians only. But Saturday Nighter has yet to work this out, just as the female Saturday Nighter has yet to work out she's dressed, well, like a man. Cut them some slack: the Saturday Nighter is still young, fresh out of school, in their first job, still thinking that anything with a giant logo is, by definition, high quality. They have much to learn.

Shops at: USC, Ted Baker, JD Sports and independent fashion boutiques nationwide.

Mr and Mrs Safe

There's nothing especially unfashionable about Mr and Mrs Safe, there's just nothing very fashionable about them either. They like to wear a nice pair of jeans, but wouldn't know an indigo dye from their elbow, which, for him, is usually clad in a nice, casual sweatshirt – the kind with a collar – or the kind of shirt that obviously wouldn't be right for the office – something in a check, for instance; for her substitute some pretty blouse, something innocuous, something, to be honest, her mother would like.

When it comes to shopping, they like a nice bit of Next or Debenhams, or Reiss if they're feeling really adventurous or they need to get a new shirt or top for a special occasion: Christmas dinner with the in-laws maybe. But most of his money goes on other things: satellite-TV subscription, a season ticket for the local team, kitchen equipment, matching mats for the company BMW, nice mugs, his small children.

They're a retailer's dream, because they represent that vast swathe of men and women in the UK who are young enough to be fashion-aware, but old enough to have spending power. But Mr and Mrs Safe are also the toughest to sell to. They have no strong opinions, no definitive tastes when it comes to clothes, and so they're never all that committed to spending when they're out shopping. He's just as happy for his wife to pick something for him. She's just as happy for her mum to buy her something.

Indeed, they are the kind of couple (they do seem to go well together) you see reading the weekend supplements, him waiting patiently outside the changing room while she does most of the spending, or her outside the shop while he looks over the latest hi-fi systems. 'It's nice,' he'll say when asked his opinion of something she has tried on. He doesn't really know what he thinks of it: if it's safe, feminine but not tarty, and not too pricey, it works for him. That's what she thinks too. They'll think about it.

Shops at: Next, Gap, Debenhams, John Lewis.

The Label Lover

She doesn't have many thoughts on fashion herself. Not any she hasn't gleaned from a cheapo weekly magazine or a celebrity snapshot at least. But, boy, can she shop – as long as it's for labels. Big, showy, statement labels that are the international currency of status for those who aspire to better themselves, superficially at least. But these statement labels are less a reflection of her appreciation of craftsmanship or creativity and more about her need to make a statement that everyone understands: 'look at me, I'm wearing Dolce & Gabbana/Gucci/Prada/whatever is the big label of the moment* [*delete as applicable], therefore I must have really arrived, I must be somebody.'

The truth is that she must really have quite a large overdraft, unless she's one of that small set who have perfected the look: footballers' wives. What is much smaller is her fashion imagination: strangely, for one so into clothes, her scope is provincial, her taste suburban. In fact, the Label Lover is something of a throwback. Back in the 1980s when designerwear was born, it was regarded as something to which to aspire for its own sake, but at the same time as something that was, frankly, a bit naff, even distasteful – designerwear was for mugs, for people who needed to wear their new wealth literally on their sleeve. Today's Label Lover wears the modern equivalent: the key garment from each new collection, the talked-about little top, the hyped heels, the super-skinny jeans. For her, each item is a point scored in an unspoken competition with another fashion slave. More than that, each item is a security blanket.

I also call this tribe the disciples of Beckham, because this is the ultimate fashion temple at which they worship. Heat magazine is their fashion bible.

Shops at: Selfridges, Harvey Nichols, Louis Vuitton, Prada Sport, Gucci, Dolce & Gabbana if they've got the cash, Karen Millen and Jane Norman if not.

The Originator

Between scruff bag and done-up is a nether world that few women can enter successfully, but which is the natural habitat of the Originator. You will rarely see her in tailoring – it's too stuffy, too ageing. But nor will you see her in track bottoms or an old sweatshirt – that's too sloppy, too childish. Rather she manages only ever to wear comfortable, casual clothing but always without looking either boring or as though she's about to pop to the supermarket or wash the car.

It is an enviable talent because it removes her from the twin pains of fashion shopping: ending up looking either too self-consciously considered or as if you really couldn't care less. And I mean really couldn't care less, not the carefree, 'I just threw this on and still manage to look fabulous' kind of couldn't-care-less of the Originator. In fact, she may make claims never to have been shopping at all. Effortless, stylish, slightly bohemian-without-the-tie-dye clothes just seem to gravitate towards her from sources that, try as you might, you won't be able to tap into yourself: a throw uncovered at a local market just outside Delhi, a blouse a friend made for her, a necklace she picked up a few years ago at some bazaar, some place …

If you didn't know better, you would imagine she was doing a Chanel: when Coco was launching No. 5, she gave small bottles of it to friends. When they returned asking her for more, she informed them that she had picked it up on holiday and could no longer recall the name of the store. Thus an insatiable demand was created. But you do know better and the fact is that the Originator not only looks elegantly unstudied, she is. She is the stuff that fashion icons, from Audrey Hepburn to Jackie Onassis to Kate Moss, are made of. There is a word women have for this kind of woman. Sadly, we cannot print it.

Shops at: anywhere and everywhere that's doing fashion right.

TRICKS OF THE TRADE

You've bought stuff before. You've browsed the rails and picked through the shelves. You've even been known to take something to the till and, miraculously, just by handing over a little piece of plastic, found that you can walk out with it. They even give you a bag to put it in. Incredible! So you think you know shops? Think again. Shops are not just rooms full of stuff you might like to buy. They are a form of entertainment. But they are also traps.

Everything about the modern store is designed to entice, to persuade you to reach for your purse. Of course, it's not the stores being entirely mendacious: we are usually willing participants in this arrangement. We want to be seduced. That's what the best stores do: of course they want to sell more clothing to people who certainly have no need for it (when was the last time you left the house naked? Exactly!). They know that all fashion is, ultimately, a luxury purchase. And they know you better than you know yourself: they know the psychology of the shopper and how best to manipulate that. In the nicest way possible, of course.

But that's also why the best stores are keen to make fashion shopping a luxury experience all round: the whole package, from the window display to the lighting, from the mood music to the fitting rooms, from the signage to the way the store is laid out and the clothes are arranged, the level of service and the people employed to serve you, even the smell of the place – all of it has been designed to make shopping rather pleasant but expensive. Or expensive but rather pleasant. You decide the order.

So before you shop, learn the tricks of the trade. It won't, sadly, make the clothes any cheaper. But it will allow you, if you choose, to cut through the spectacle and pizzazz and make a genuinely independent decision as to whether you really, really need another black jacket, or whether you've been lured by the lovely seduction of fashion shopping.

The UK's top ten department stores account for 90 per cent of the nation's entire department-store business.

Windows – through the looking glass

It pays to advertise

Strangely, there was a time when shops did not have shop windows, at least not as we now know them. They had windows to let in light, but they did not have windows as selling tools. And that's what the window is. It sets the stage. Of course, many shops are brands in their own right these days – sophisticated shoppers know what they represent and what they are likely to sell without having to see them, and this applies to local independent stores as much as major international names. But there are plenty that are not.

So, first and foremost, the window is their advertising space: it gives a snapshot of what lies inside. It may highlight new collections or trends and in doing so it is providing shoppers with the kind of information they may glean from flicking through a fashion magazine: this is what's happening, and this is where you can buy it. In other words, the shop window is a form of advertising.

Show me the money

As in all advertising, big budgets go a long way, for instance in terms of the quality of the materials used in the display. The more ornate the display, the more important it appears – we dedicated shoppers pay close attention to window displays. So a display that looks great from far away – say, the other side of the road – looks very different when our noses are pressed up against the window. One that suddenly reveals itself as having been made, *Blue Peter*-style, out of a couple of loo-roll tubes and a washing-up bottle will not impress.

In fact, the attention paid to the basics of a window – cleanliness, tidiness, well-looked-after props and so on – are a good indication of just how good a shop this is, or isn't as the case may be. This isn't a guaranteed rule of thumb: go to some cities and the side-street independent store with a window display that hasn't been dusted for half a century can occasionally mask a veritable treasure trove within. But it's usually right.

It's, like, conceptual man

But big budgets are not the be-all and end-all of a window that gets your attention – that lies in the concept. It may be as simple as a window in which the display is minimalist, but the products in it change every day, making every journey past on the way to work a fight with a new temptation. Or it may be all about the three key aspects of shop-window display: good humour, off-the-wall-ness and the surreal approach. Look out for these when you shop. You won't have to look far – you'll find that you're automatically drawn to them because they will either make you smile, or stop to try and work out what the hell is going on.

The best retailers know, however, that if they stick too closely to the theme that the fashion they're highlighting somehow suggests (for instance, roll out the old scooter whenever fashion gets Modish) there is always the risk that other shops will do the same. And then you won't be able to remember one shop from another. The best props, in other words, may not seem relevant to the clothes on display, but, reading between the lines, might offer some kind of comment. Well, it gets you thinking ...

La Rinascente department store in Milan once had a window dresser named Giorgio Armani. He went on to work in fashion, apparently.

The five worst crimes of a window dresser

1 Autumn leaves: you know the score. It's the new autumn collections. And what better way to show them off than wonderful leaf motifs, vinyls and graphics in the windows. Not.

2 New season, new you: so many retailers try to convince us that buying a new top at the start of the new season will change our lives. Silly straplines like this are just lazy. Don't be fooled.

3 Hearts and flowers: Valentine's Day is bigger than ever these days on our high streets. Chocolates, flowers and lingerie all run out of the door. But do we really have to put up with the cheesy windows to go with it all?

4 The poster: sometimes blown-up imagery can look fantastic, sometimes it's as boring as batshit. So much more clever and cool to take fuller advantage of the three-dimensional nature of windows to tell a much bigger story.

5 Ding-dong merrily: have you ever been to New York at Christmas to see their fantastic window displays? Christmas should be the most magical time of the year for our shops. Retailers who stick a bit of old twig and glitter in the window ought to be shot.

Abracadabra!

When used cleverly in a window, colour can be extremely emotive (blues are cool, reds are warm) but also suggestive (red is sexy, black is chic, brown cosy and autumnal, yellow free-spirited and summery). They can highlight a garment by picking up the tiniest detail in it.

Light, too, is important in setting the tone. On sunny days blinds are used too increase the intensity of the artificial lighting. At night this artificial light is dimmed so that it doesn't saturate all the colours in the clothing. That said, a flat light may be directed straight at a garment in a way that diffuses colour and texture but highlights its real sales point – its shape. Light a garment from both above and below and it eliminates shadow, resulting in a very clean presentation. Lighting black clothing with blue light makes it look more luxurious, while a red dress lit with red light will seem all the more intense.

Similarly, clever styling can massively increase the appeal of a piece of clothing by exaggerating its essence, be that its skinniness, cosiness, sparkliness or luxuriousness. Always check out how much an outfit has been pinned by the window dresser before leaping into the changing room with it, as you will often find that, in reality, it has a completely different silhouette. The best displays also always show outfits styled in a way that could walk right out of the window. Creative does not equal wacky. Few people are sold by the 'tights worn as scarf' or 'belt worn as necklace' school of styling.

Robert Rauschenberg, James Rosenquist, Jasper Johns and Andy Warhol – leading artists of the Pop Art style – all began their artistic careers as window dressers. Oh, and me.

It's theatre, darling

But the window also represents the store itself. The window is, in large part, the face of the store. And just as you might judge anyone by their face – is this person approachable, is this person crazed? – so you do with a store. The window is what tells you whether this is the kind of store you want to go into.

Consequently, contemporary window displays often do not simply arrange some natty clothes on mannequins and let the product do the talking. Sometimes a bold window display will be completely devoid of clothes or accessories or anything else to buy altogether; instead, it will simply set a mood. Indeed, the window display is now more like an art installation or a fashion shoot in a magazine, without the freedom to airbrush a two-dimensional image to perfection – it's clever, witty, sumptuous or theatrical, promising a clever, witty, sumptuous or theatrical experience inside. And every shopkeeper wants their window to be different and individual, hence distinctive and memorable. That is not easy to pull off.

Surrealist Salvador Dali designed shop windows for New York store Bonwit Teller. Dali's design included mannequins that cried tears of blood, propped up in baths full of mud and surrounded by suspended hands, each holding a mirror. Nobody understood it then either. Even though controversy can work in a window display, the store hated it and had it disassembled. As it was taken down, Dali managed to let a bath slip through the window. Oops.

Pavement power

The window has to get your attention not only in competition with all the other things that are fighting for it, be that billboards or the urban environment, but also in competition with other media, from TV to the radio and the internet, much of which can utilise the latest high-techery to get your attention. It also has to compete with other shops where you may choose to spend your money.

And it has to do all this as you're pounding past through the rain under an umbrella; it has to do this as you whiz by in a car, especially because most of the people passing by a shop window are not thinking about shopping. Crazy, I know. So no wonder I encourage many of my clients to spend on their windows as it's the most cost effective and powerful way to speak to the customer.

I call this pavement power. Or the power of a window to stop you in your tracks even if, as is usually the case, your head is quite simply elsewhere.

Those people you see tiptoeing around in their socks in the window area, with a few pins poking out of the corners of their mouths, they're brilliant stylists. When you see a window installed beautifully, think Harvey Nichols, think Liberty, think French Connection, think Zara – these are the people who make us stop and take notice. And that is just as powerful, just as involving as any advertising campaign

But either way, what they do is not as simple or as naive as it may look. It's especially fun to watch the stores sweat it out in December, trying to be festive without being clichéd, or try to promote their sales without looking tacky. Many fail miserably.

But you be the judge. Vote not only with your purse, but also with your opinion. Does the window work? Does that certain shade of blue speak of serenity or of chilliness? Is the display enticing or confusing?

Get it right and the best windows are a form of entertainment in their own right. Would 'window shopping' exist as a phenomenon if windows were dull and lifeless and full of just posters? I doubt it.

How to read a window

Did that window stop me in my tracks? Did it stand out from the rest on the high street? If so, it's done its job, whatever you think of its style or content. Here's what to look out for:

Visual puns: a fun way of attracting your attention, like my 'Peas on Earth' Christmas window – I stuffed the window with hundreds of massive green peas. Bonkers, I know, but attention-grabbing.

Artful decay: because that's cool on the street, right, homies?

Art: so in vogue at the moment, from photography to installation. Not only does it massage our ego (as it assumes we understand and relate to it), but it's also great exposure for the artists.

The single product in isolation: the item as star, in the spotlight. So it has to be good, right? Works well with, say, a Comme des Garçons dress or a Hermes scarf, where the product speaks for itself.

Balance of 3D and 2D: gives depth to a window, making the total effect seem bigger than it otherwise would.

Specially commissioned artwork: this is a store with the budgets and power, but let's hope they spend the money on service too.

Distorted mannequins: grotesque or highly stylised, the age of the standard, nylon-haired mannequin staring into the middle distance is so over.

Captions and phrases: snappy lines or challenging thoughts can add gravitas to a pair of tights if done well. Imagine huge words in colourful, bold letters saying 'STOP!' or 'HOT!'.

Prop as icon: they reflect the desirable essence of the fashion item.

Bold use of a single colour or blocks of primary colours: always eye-catching.

Irrelevant props: or are they? Stop and think about it, then go and buy something.

Stacking or repetition: piles of products may sometimes be hard to decipher, but always suggest that the store has a lot to offer if only you'd go inside. I love the power of 16 red T-shirts, one after the other. Now that's confident.

Space: because a shop window doesn't have to be full of stuff and sometimes the less crowded it is, the more the items within it have impact.

Scale: grand and imposing, but big is not necessarily better.

Slanted light: creates an outdoor mood or scene.

Linear or vertical arrangements: they're trying to draw your eye to some part of the window where … ooh, that's a nice dress …

Feathers: what display stylists call avant-garde, with items bought specifically to add interest to the window but that are not expected to sell.

The everyday and the expensive: one makes the other look even more fabulous.

Glamour put in the shade: suggests that the item in the limelight is more glamorous still.

Cold lighting: creates a dark, more dramatic tone.

Clashing pattern: you may not want to wear it, but it looks good in a window.

Mannequins: are not just mannequins but are made seasonally to reflect new styles of clothes and new ways of wearing them.

To serve, or not to serve …

For all the razzmatazz of the modern fashion store, even for the most excellent selection of clothes, what can really turn a mundane shopping experience into an excellent one, or a mundane one into a truly depressing one, is the service.

The collapse of a service culture in the UK over recent years has come, ironically, in line with the rise of the service industries. Whether it be sub-contracting to faraway call centres, cutting back on staff training or a general disempowering of the people who deal direct with the customer, why is it so few people are ready to take responsibility for the customer they are dealing with? Service is a dying art. It is easy to complain, of course. And that's the problem – it is all too easy to complain. Standards are terrible. There's a lot to complain about.

The best retailers understand that sales staff are central to any fashion shopper's experience of a store. For all the wonderful windows and the great layout, the real experience of that brand lies in the interaction we have with the sales staff. All retail is a people business, so it's essential that the sales staff have conviction in the company they work for and the products they sell in order to convince us shoppers to spend our money.

Creating such conviction in fashion-retail companies that sometimes have hundreds or thousands of staff is no small challenge. But that is what has to be done: wages, hours, benefits, a sense of being part of a team, a management that understands

and is not aloof – all these factors play a part in making sales staff better at their job and in reducing staff turnover, which is notoriously high in retail and especially in fashion retail. This is just one reason why some businesses fail to invest in training – why bother if the trainees are going to leave soon? But the lack of training is more likely to make them leave. They need this to understand the culture of the fashion store. If they can't understand it, how are us shoppers likely to?

If, as a shopper, you want an indication of a good store with good service, just see how many faces you recognise from your last visit. The higher the number, the better the store and the business behind it probably is.

The best sales staff think like us shoppers. This can't be difficult. Take off the name badge and give them a day off and they become shoppers. Yet it is remarkable how few good sales staff there are. The good ones are in high demand.

This is why independents so often win out over multiples or department stores: on the shopfloor you can often find yourself dealing direct with the owner/manager, someone who is not only naturally incentivised to make your experience the best possible, but who also has the best knowledge of their stock (they are probably also the buyer or work closely with them) and can make

Good service can transform a mundane shopping experience into an excellent one.

on-the-spot decisions if you press for some kind of discount. And why not? This is your opportunity to strike a deal: their commitment to shave a few pounds off their margin in return for your commitment to buy several items. And then, so bowled over by the unusually good service, probably come back with friends in tow. After all, how often have you felt yourself developing an instant guilt complex that has pushed you into buying something you may otherwise not have bought? And all just because the assistant has been sooo helpful.

When you find good service, support it: write and congratulate the store, inform the manager, vote with your purse. When it's bad, vote with your feet. There are very few stores now selling an item that cannot be found elsewhere. It may be an inconvenience, but these stores won't improve until their sales figures give them reason to take action to do so. Besides, you pay for service. It's part of the margin built into the ticket price. If you don't get good service, you are effectively being ripped off (see chapter 6 for more on this).

Closing the deal

At the end of the sale, the clever shop will need to move to the bit where they take your money. We call this 'closing the sale'. Fashion stores, like most others, are full of promotions and deals that encourage 'closure'. It might be a free tie with two shirts, a percentage off shoes if you buy them with a dress, or a pair of sunnies with your optical frames if you buy them on the same day. Some of these deals really work and make us spend more money. Some are random and badly thought through. Next time you are out, have a look round and judge for yourself.

The selling tribes

I have spent long enough in shops to classify those who serve or don't serve us into tribes, from those who consistently deliver formidable service to the downright rude and unhelpful. If you work in a shop, see if you can spot your tribe in my list. And if you're a shopper, name them and shame them. It's the only way they'll get better.

Eager Eva

'Can I help you, madam?'
'No, thank you, I'm just looking.'

'These jeans have got 3 per cent elastane in them,' she tells you. 'Elastane is stretchy stuff,' she goes on. 'It helps you get into them. Not that you'll need it,' she quickly adds. All of which would possibly be of interest, if you weren't looking for a cardigan.

Eager Eva may not be paid by commission, but you would never know it. She is the first person to bound to your side the second you have entered the shop, to enquire how you are and whether she can help – which you momentarily take to be genuine friendliness until (a) you realise that she says this to everyone in exactly the same chirpy manner and (b) she asks you for the tenth time. This is what it must feel like to be a celebrity and have a stalker. At every moment Eager Eva is at your elbow with some titbit of information about the item you apparently didn't even have to touch (you think you may have just glanced towards it, by accident) in order to be giving signs of interest in buying.

A trip to the fitting room entails a running commentary on your choice's suitability along with the offer of half the store's merchandise as possible 'co-ordinating separates', as she calls them. None of them seems to co-ordinate. Staying any longer becomes unbearable. You leave empty handed.

Where you'll find her:
at the shop door ready to pounce.

Chatty Cathy

Cathy talks a lot. Unfortunately it's on the phone to her friends. She knows a lot. Unfortunately it's not about service.

You've been at the till for two minutes now, waiting to pay. And she still hasn't even acknowledged you. Still she keeps chatting. Eventually she breaks off from her conversation, somewhat reluctantly and with what you're sure was a bit of a tut, and raises an eyebrow in your direction: 'Yes?'. It's perfectly obvious what you want – to hand over your money and leave. But you're wondering now whether to give your money to some other store. She tells her friend she'll have to call her back. It is a great inconvenience. Don't you realise that she is not here to help you? Don't you realise who she is? Or rather, who she could be, if only she could get out of this town, or even just this shop?

Chatty Cathy, you see, is all just a bit above sales or service. She is the kind who sizes you up as you enter the store to assess your fashionability and your wealth, as if you needed to demonstrate sufficient amounts of both even to set foot over the threshold. She is the kind who looks disdainfully if you touch the clothes, as though your hand were covered with manure. Even as you hand over your hard-earned cash, Chatty Cathy can't quite bring herself to look you in the eyes.

It is all a desperate power trip for her. It makes her feel secure to know that, as she stands there in her chichi outfit – the one she has to wear, quite possibly the only one she has to wear – she is somehow several stations above you. In her darker moments, she thinks of service as being demeaning: after all, she is a designer too. She doesn't just work in fashion. She is fashion. And as far as she's concerned, you're just cluttering up the shop. It is time for you to leave. And never to go back.

Where you'll find her:
behind the cash desk or next to the phone. Basically as far away from the sales floor as possible.

Don't-know Darren

'Do you have this top in any other colours?' 'Dunno.'
'Do you have this in another size?' 'Dunno.'
'Could you get it from another store?' 'Can't do that.'
'Could it be ordered in?' 'Don't think so.'

Don't-know Darren is a paragon of the unhelpful and, more frustratingly, the unthinking. When people speak of great service as having 'gone the extra mile', Don't-know Darren goes the extra inch – backwards. Clearly he has never undergone any kind of staff training. What is more incredible still is how he ever got a job in sales in the first place. He is almost pathologically unsuited: he really has no interest in clothes and even less interest in you. He lacks charisma – even the faux variety some sales staff can turn on – and has no initiative: if it means making an enquiry on your behalf, or going to the stockroom, or even offering an alternative to the garment he doesn't have in your size or colour, well, it's easier just to say no. The faster he gets to his tea break, the better.

The bottom line? He doesn't want to help because he just does not care whether you leave the store as a customer who is satisfied or suicidal. And talking of bottom lines … Given that the success of many stores is often measured in terms of their takings per square metre, Don't-know Darren is literally a waste of space. The spot on which he stands would be better given over to another rack of clothes. The rack would probably be more helpful too.

Where you'll find him:

lurking in a corner somewhere. Or manning a telephone helpline. Don't-know Darren without a face is just about as painful as this tribe gets. You know the type. The kind who ruin your day without even knowing it. Don't-know Darren, your time is up. You've been evicted.

Spot-on Suzy

Some say she is mythical. Others that they saw her once, but they didn't have their glasses on and it was a bit foggy that day. But somewhere out there is Spot-on Suzy, the ultimate fashion sales person.

Spot-on Suzy is everything Don't-know Darren, Chatty Cathy and Eager Eva are not: she is friendly – I mean, in a way you believe; she is at hand without being cloying; she knows her stock inside and out and even inside-out; she has a stylist's eye as to what goes with what. Let's not be naive enough to think that she utilises these skills out of the goodness of her heart: she is there to sell clothes. But she can sell clothes that, although you may not have realised it, really do suit you and that you'll really enjoy wearing. That's a real talent: to encourage you to explore the kind of clothing that, until that moment, you were closed off to.

If she hasn't got your size, she'll do all she can to track it down. If she can't do that, her suggestion for an alternative will be a good one. As a last resort, she may – and this is the real acid test – direct you to a competitor's store. Why? Because she wants not just your money, but also your trust. She wants you to come back and to be able to ask for her by name. And she knows that if you look good, that's not only a good advertisement for the store, that's good enough reason to do so. Sold.

Where you'll find her:

Spot-on Suzy was born to work in shops. You'll find her in all your favourite shops. She will be one of the main reasons you've gone back.

Shopability

Just because the windows have been sufficiently enticing to get you through the door does not mean that you will find what you want once you are inside. How you move around the shop floor is determined by how good the merchandising is. Do you know what a merchandiser is? Sounds boring, but this is one of the most essential jobs in a store. A bad merchandiser makes for a bad shop. A good one makes shopping a dream.

Shopability is my word for what it sounds like. The ability to shop easily, be guided and inspired. Like a bee drawn to flowers, a good shop, put together by a good merchandiser, will pull you this way and that without you even noticing. You think you're in control, you're just browsing. Let me let you into a secret, your every move in a well-merchandised shop was pre-determined from the minute the window made you stop and go inside.

And when a shop gets it really right, I call it the pinball effect. Imagine yourself pulled back on a firm steel coil and released to bounce among departments. Then go to Topshop on Oxford Circus in London and see it happen for real.

The best shops of all offer a perfect pace between parts of the shop that are jaw-droppingly amazing and other parts that are quieter and more suited to browsing.

When merchandising is bad, and you can't find the product you're looking for, it's probably not because it isn't there. It's just because you can't find it: there is often so much stock on the shopfloor – dozens of lookalike styles, with several of every size imaginable – that shops are often more akin to a jungle made of wool and cotton. Or, there's just one of each item on display like a holy relic that you can worship but must not touch. Then you must go through the often tortuous process of finding someone to find your size, for which they disappear to the stockroom, sometimes never to return.

Good fashion stores are examples of the art of what retailers call merchandising or visual merchandising: the way clothes are displayed on racks and shelves, and the way these in turn are arranged to make the store as easily navigated as possible. Even the racks and shelves have been carefully considered: to be adaptable, for instance, so that even if the stock is getting old and tired, the way it is presented can be reinvigorated; while their quality is both a reflection of the (supposed) quality of product sold on them and of the money made by those products. A cheap rack usually holds cheap clothes.

The way those clothes are put on the rack, however, can make or break not only the fashion store's image, but also the determination of us shoppers to find what we want. The 'pile it high, sell it cheap' store makes no bones about art and so we accept cheap clothes sold cheaply, just as we expect expensive clothes to be treated with more respect (this is one reason why sale time is such a fraught one when it comes to controlling the image of upmarket stores). Clever chain stores can sell cheaper clothes in a way that makes them look aspirational. In short, there are usually less of these items. Unfortunately this means staff are always busy tidying or restocking – too busy to help us customers in other words.

It is the middle market where many fashion stores run aground: not-inexpensive clothing cheapened by being crammed on to racks, one style hiding another. Whether true or not, it also suggests disorganisation and poor management. In a strange way, sometimes less choice equals more choice – a more focused, better-edited selection means you're more likely to find something you want and feel that the shop has done the hard work for you.

More than 25 per cent of shoppers think that designer items are overpriced. No, really?

The art of display

Touch me, feel me – touch is a key aspect of sales. Watch other shoppers as they wander around the store. They are not only looking at, but handling the goods too. This is even more the case with fashion, in which texture can be so important, both style wise and in terms of how we assess the quality and value of a garment. It's one reason why fashion shopping over the internet is a smaller market than that for, say, books or CDs. So the best fashion stores allow you access to the clothing without having to reach, stoop or ask a sales assistant to unlock a cabinet. Half the time you're only looking, so don't want to bother them. But then again, if you don't get a closer look and touch the item, how are you ever going to be converted from browser to hey, big spender?

Take a look – the most profitable products are placed not only at eye-level, but also at the eye-level of a particular kind of shopper. So if the item is usually bought by a woman – a skirt, for instance – it will be placed at the eye-level of an average-height woman; the same applies to clothing for men. Consequently, in fashion stores shelves have been found to be more effective sales tools than traditional floor-standing racks. Tables have also become a popular way of merchandising clothes – because tables are associated with eating, they are thought to be 'comfort zones' that make us shoppers feel at ease.

Hot spots – product on promotion in a store is generally positioned in a place retailers call a hot spot. Hot because it's visible from the door, well lit, easy to linger in front of, well signposted and hopefully replenished regularly. Hot spots without any product are just plain annoying.

How shops make more money

It sounds obvious, but not all shops have really thought about it.
To make more money out of us, shops can do three things.

1 Sell the same product to the customer, but do it more profitably (raise the price).

2 Sell more products to the customer through promotion (so they spend more and come back more often).

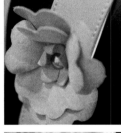

3 Find a new customer (and sell to them as well).

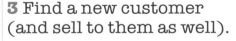

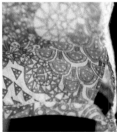

Layout lore

You are not a lab rat, invited into a maze through which you must head for the cheese. But store layout is a science that thinks you're a lab rat. We all know why shops put small, less expensive things by the till: they hope that when you're there paying for your big item, the buzz will be sufficient to convert that excess adrenalin into an additional, unplanned purchase. We've all done it. Back home 'What the hell' becomes 'What the hell did I buy that for?'.

Fashion retailers use tricks that are no less effective, but perhaps rather more subtle. They understand the dynamics of traffic flow – the way the racks and shelves are mapped out – in order to encourage you to pass through the entire store, not only past all their lovely goodies but directly to what are called 'destination products'. These are the goods that offer the greatest profit or that they deem most likely to sell. It's all about getting the most from every square metre of the store, and making the store as easy as possible for you to spend your money in. Like people, stores have a basic anatomy. Let me take you through it:

At the door – this area is known as the 'decompression zone'. It is where you take stock of the new environment in which you find yourself, take your coat off, shake your umbrella, and pause to assess the situation. If it's either too empty or too cluttered, it can dissuade people from moving further inside. It is the least profitable of any area of the shop, but the area immediately afterwards is often the most profitable. This may explain your tendency to buy 'the first thing you see'. That is quite literal. Your hunter-gatherer instinct tweaked, you have primed yourself to buy. The most appealing items – the most fashionable, the best value, the newest stock – consequently go at the front of the store. I spend much of my time going in and out of shops and am constantly amazed how little time retailers themselves spend pretending to be shoppers. First impressions really do count. They so often forget that a bad smell, fag butts, naff music or a general feeling of unpleasantness are often all it takes for most of us to turn on our heels and walk straight out.

■ *'Fashion is what one wears oneself. What is unfashionable is what other people wear.' Oscar Wilde* ■

A few steps on – now you have entered what is called the 'strike zone'. This is typically to the right of the entrance as you face the store, because western people (perhaps because most of us are right-handed) have a tendency to move to the right of a store on entering. Here fashion retailers like to set the tone: they will place items that give an indication of the kind of store they are – whether high street or high fashion, designer or basics – as well as the kind of prices they offer. Here will be placed items that are not so overly expensive as to be off-putting, but not misleadingly cheap either. The strike zone tends to be full of attractively affordable clothes.

Into the store – once firmly within the store, the retailer's most valuable clothes (not the most expensive, but those that offer the store the highest margin and the highest rate of sales) are typically placed along the right wall. These tend not to be so-called 'demand' items – those that you had decided to buy before you had even entered the store, be that a pair of tights or a three-pack of thongs. Rather, they are the items of 'seduction' – the ones that had not been on your hit list until you saw them. Retailers are aware that your interest level diminishes the longer you are in the store, or about five minutes on if you're male. They need to net your purse quickly.

A room with a view? – us shoppers prefer to be able to see all around the store from wherever we're standing, to know where certain sections are and see how to get there, so retailers are careful not to place units where they block our line of sight. This draws us on through the store, from one promotional hot spot – a clearly signposted selection of bargain clothes – to another towards the back of the store.

At the back – here, at what is known as the 'destination area', is where the fashion shops place all the high-demand items – the so-called 'must-haves', the fast-fashion garments and the clothes you saw in the window, just as supermarkets always put the milk at the back. Why? Because it draws you to the rear of the store and makes sure you see everything else they have on offer en route. Similarly, in large stores the main thoroughfares will be lined with what is deemed the most saleable products. Close your eyes and run as you use these aisles.

To the till – tills have tended to be centrally located, not simply for convenience (wherever you are, it is the smallest journey to the 'please pay here' sign) but rather because, wherever you are, it means passing additional merchandise before you finally get to the till. These days more stores are placing the till point to the left of the entrance: it encourages a full anti-clockwise sweep of the store before finally ending up at the till. This is also where all those small, impulse items are most abundant. Why here? Because you are a captive audience. Queuing takes time. While in line, the eyes wander the immediate vicinity. Even if there is no queue, card transactions and wrapping all buy time for you to make an additional last-minute purchase.

The more relaxed you are, the more likely you are to part with your readies.

Welcome!

Or why some stores draw you in and others turn you off.

Fashion stores are much more than places simply to buy clothes. They aim to offer an all-round pleasant experience, whether you buy anything or not. Competition is so fierce that anything they can do to get you through their door and not another store's is now high on their agenda. And the more effort they make, the higher the bar is raised and the greater our expectations. In part this is because brands, especially fashion ones, have switched their thinking away from just being purveyors of clothing to being providers of an entire lifestyle.

In turn, the flagship stores of top fashion brands especially set out to make their stores a complete brand environment – stepping over their thresholds is to step into a new world that entirely reflects that brand's ethos, be it edginess, glamour, fun, rather like entering either a pounding nightclub, a refined, traditional gentleman's club, a temple to chic minimalism or a kind of home from home. This has placed added pressure on department stores and independents to be equally inventive in the atmosphere they create around the clothes they sell, from the signage to the lighting, from the music to the smell of the place.

All this is especially true for women. It is changing, but male shoppers typically want the fastest route to finding the product they want, with the minimum of fuss, and then to exit the store as quickly as possible. This isn't because they don't enjoy shopping: they're just more goal-oriented. Given the encouragement, women prefer to linger, especially over clothing. But the encouragement has to be there.

Get it right and shops become palaces of consumption. Get it wrong and, well, there's always another shop around the corner.

Average shopping times
(according to a study):

Woman with man: 4 minutes, 41 seconds
Woman alone: 5 minutes, 2 seconds
Woman with female companion:
8 minutes, 51 seconds

Light fantastic

Lighting is functional – it may be fun shopping for clothes in the dark, but tasteful co-ordination may then go out of the window. More than this, lighting is what gives a store its atmosphere: if it's ambient in a supermarket, in a fashion store it should be theatrical. Uplighting can ruin a store display because it creates sinister shadows in all the wrong places. As shoppers, we naturally feel more comfortable with lighting coming from above, because this mimics the sun. But it takes a multitude of low-wattage lighting in different positions – from the side or from behind as much as from above – to show off the characteristics of the clothes.

A light is not just a light in other words, especially when it comes to setting the tone of a fashion store – strip lighting isn't welcoming in any place other than a supermarket, while too soft a light and you're not sure what you're trying on – or highlighting the quality of clothing. Compact fluorescent, incandescent, high-intensity definition, quartz halogen ... and these are just the types of bulb that can be used to create different effects, according to their intensity and position. Fluorescent, for instance, suggests utility, while incandescent gives a store a more traditional feel.

Lighting also enhances colour, which is among the most primitive but effective prompts for you to reach for your purse. Like babies and sparkly things, even grown-ups are drawn towards brighter colours: people will buy more of vibrantly coloured products. This may not apply to fashion, where our sensibility is muted by seasons, current trends, colour associations and a long-lasting love of black, but it does explain why colour is used so heavily in packaging, on carrier bags and for in-store decoration. Just as, regardless of cut or fabric, we are more ready to associate a red dress with sexiness, a navy one with sobriety and so on, so we associate a dark fashion-store interior with sophistication, a white one with cleanliness, freshness and simplicity, and so on.

The sweet smell of excess

Fashion stores of today are multi-sensory experiences, and that includes your nose. I'm not talking about the chemical fog you have to wade through to get beyond the cosmetics section of your local department store. It's cleverer than that. Just as car dealerships have been known to use a 'new car smell' spray to enhance the sense of cleanliness of their vehicles, and supermarkets often place their bakeries near the most popular entrance in order to lure in customers with a 'fresh bread' aroma, so fashion stores are starting to do so with clothes. Shoe stores, for instance, may pump out the smell of leather to enhance the shopper's sense of the quality materials used, while others may feed a 'just laundered' smell out through the air conditioning.

And because smell works in such a deeply subliminal way, its influence on you can be powerful without you even being aware of it. Some stores are now developing 'aromarketing' that simply aims to create a sense of well-being by, for instance, using nostalgic smells that may remind you of your childhood. The idea is that it makes you feel secure and so relaxed. And the more relaxed you are, the more likely you are to part with your readies. Like you need any more encouragement.

Major department stores can receive almost 1000 new items of stock each day – just think of all those new shopping opportunities that brings.

Where am I going to?

Look carefully and you'll see fashion shops are full of signs: information about departments or discounts, special offers or new collections. All of them can be very useful, or utterly pointless. Shoppers are impatient these days – they don't really want to wait for a sales assistant to point them in the right direction. An open-plan store, as most large fashion stores are now, requires all the necessary info to be out in the open too.

But not all signs are effective because they don't ask what each shopper is doing in that spot and whether the info is relevant. Or they put a lot of info on a sign in a place where the shopper is likely to be on the move – because a sign in the wrong place is worse than no sign at all if it ends up misdirecting. The most effective signs, in terms of getting noticed, are those that interrupt the shopper's view across the shop floor. Normally this would be an annoyance – unless it's providing some useful info, like where the hell the changing rooms are, when all is forgiven. Stores can have too many signs, meaning that they look cluttered or become a distraction – after all, how many times do you need to be told that there is a sale on?

Shop signs have to be punchy too and work while we stay on the move: most of us will only glance towards a sign. We're more interested in the clothes, dummy. In that couple of seconds the message has to be given or we just stroll on.

Still, it's better than being insulted. Stores that insist on telling you the stringent conditions by which you can and cannot take clothes into the changing room, or to wait before entering – wait, that is, for the sales assistant to get back from where he or she shouldn't be – are dinosaurs in the world of modern shopping. Tell me what to do and the first thing I'll do is shop elsewhere!

Some 93 per cent of people spend more money than they planned to when they go shopping. No surprises there then.

Music, maestro

Music can be used to delineate a boundary or create a space in a fashion store – modern speaker technology allows it to be targeted at specific areas, so the music acts as cue that you have now left one area and entered another, a trick often used by the different concessions within a department store. Music also sets the mood. It can equally drive you to distraction if it's too loud, too intrusive, too bland or too clichéd, rolling out Nat King Cole every Christmas.

But music is such an integral part of the fashion-store experience – imagine the unwelcoming sense of chill that would descend on you if you walked into a store to be faced with absolute silence – that store designers even position the walls according to how well they absorb sound. And don't believe that music has no influence on you, short of the fact that you're more likely to stay in a shop playing a tune you like or exit one playing a tune you don't. Although you may not even be consciously listening to it, certain types of music will make you feel more upbeat and, guess what, spend more as a result. Big fashion chains consequently control the music they have piped through the speakers very carefully. When they play, you pay.

A room of one's own

Everyone has experienced the nightmare of the ill-conceived fitting room. The worst offence (because it would take a monkey with a screwdriver and five minutes in B&Q to remedy) is the lack of a hook on which, most importantly, to hang your own clothes, let alone the ones you're trying on. It says a lot about the retailer's high regard for his products that he's happy for you to leave them on the floor while you change. A lack of space is almost as bad. And having to leave the changing room to see what you look like – and be assaulted with the robotic compliments of the sales staff – is one way for retailers to cut down on sales. If you can't easily find a mirror, or can't even find the changing rooms, too often you just won't bother. Who can blame you?

There is no good explanation as to why so many fashion stores under-estimate the value of good changing rooms – it's been proven that the better the changing room, the higher the sales. According to one study, the likelihood of us buying something increases by half if there is interaction with a sales assistant, and by 100 per cent if there is interaction and use of the dressing room, which drives home their importance. Maybe some retailers don't want to waste space that could be given over to displaying more clothes, or maybe they consider changing rooms to be out of sight and thus not part of the store's image. They couldn't be more wrong: it's in the changing room where the deal is clinched. That's where you make your decision to buy.

Assuming, that is, you can even stand to be in it for long enough. The most unpleasant aspect of any bad fitting room is lighting. This, admittedly, requires considerable investment on the part of the retailer to blend lighting for the best overall effect. Too harsh a light and all one experiences is not the clothes but a sharp, crystal clear, no blemish-left-unrevealed reminder of one's greasy skin/orange peel arse/expanding gut – the association of feeling bad with the product one is trying on will almost certainly be made. And that's one less sale.

Alternatively, using the best, that is to say the most flattering lighting – the bulb equivalent of candlelight – may make you look like a movie star but will give the least accurate representation of the clothes you're trying on. You may end up buying, only later to find out that, miraculously, the top you bought has changed colour on the way home. Be warned.

Bags of style

It may be more than a little naff, but it's a testament to the power of fashion brands that some people use their carrier bags long after they have carried that lovely pair of shoes home. At least this suggests that the bag is sturdy enough to get further use. Some people even collect the bags – with nothing in them. What's that about? Yet so many fashion stores are a let-down with their bags: they're flimsy, so that the handle starts to sag with anything less than featherweight inside; the handles are too long, so the only option is to carry them over the shoulder, or drag them along the ground like the kill from a hunt; they're the wrong size, so you end up using a bag you could pack your entire wardrobe in for just a pair of knickers, skulking somewhere in a corner; they're made of paper, which is to be applauded from an ecological standpoint, but, if the paper is too thin, dissolves in a downpour.

The better fashion stores have realised that their bags are representative of their brand, with most aspiring to seem sophisticated and upmarket. Most shoppers want to keep feeling that too as they travel on with their new purchase, which is why emblazoning 'sale!' all over them is an utterly dumb idea. Perhaps the shopper wants to feel proud that they have shopped at a certain store. What they certainly don't want to feel – even if they're a seasoned seeker of bargains – is cheap. Sometimes it's better to stuff your purchase into an old supermarket carrier bag than to become a mobile advertising hoarding for someone's end-of-season mark-down sale.

American department store Bloomingdale's introduced the first 'designer' shopping bag in 1961. The store commissioned artist Joseph Kinigstein to create a bag that, daringly for the time, omitted the store's name.

WHEN TO SHOP

Truly dedicated followers of fashion will know there's a time to shop and a time not to shop. Though trends come and go, the fashion year follows a strict timetable, season by season. Learn when is the best time to nab a bargain, and when to be first through the doors to get the new season's look, hot off the catwalk.

Month by month

January

Crack open that thick wad of virgin fifties, flex those credit cards, and prepare to regret overspending for the next three months. Yes, it's sale time. Actually, if the year has been a bad one for the high street (listen to those business reports on the radio during the previous autumn), many stores, especially department stores, will have marked down much of their stock in December, in advance of the official first day of the sales. Although retailers will hope to have had a boom time during the Christmas period, with more people shopping online and even postponing Christmas shopping precisely to wait for the sales, bargains are increasingly there to be had. Often stores now operate a little-advertised clearance department all year round – this is where the unwanted sale items go.

Watch out though – not all stores will have the previous autumn/winter's fashion items on sale: some will even stockpile those items from previous seasons' sales that failed to sell last time around. For some shoppers that's an opportunity to pick up the much wanted piece they had missed first time around. For others, it can make for a disappointing sale. Note, also, that different stores run their sales in different ways and over different times. Some make a single mark-down. Others will mark down progressively throughout their sale period, leaving you gambling on whether to pay now or hold on for a better price and risk losing out altogether (on the whole, stores will not 'hold' or 'put by' sale items).

Just as important as when the sales start (refer to your local paper for details because some stores will hold off until as late as mid-January) are the less publicised dates of when they finish. Some stores play this by ear: if they calculate that their floor space would get a better return by cutting their losses and getting the new season's merchandise out, a sale can end suddenly overnight. Beware, bargain hunters!

And get excited, fashion hunters! Of course, after the sales come the new collections. Mid- to late January is when most stores will be unveiling these (though if you are after a specific item in short supply you should phone around to find out just which stockists will be putting out their deliveries first). This is the time of the year to sign on to store databases in order to be notified of future key dates and deliveries.

After the sales come the new collections.

January also sees the designers take to the catwalks. Milan holds the menswear shows around the middle of the month, showing the collections that will be in the shops the following autumn/winter. From about the 20th of the month, Paris stops for the haute-couture shows (that's the really expensive stuff), followed by its own menswear shows.

There is a saying that you should never go grocery shopping on an empty stomach or mattress shopping when you're tired. Neither should you go clothes shopping when you're naked. Especially in winter.

February

There's no point waiting any longer. Most of the mainline spring/
summer merchandise is now out on the sales floor, including
so-called 'cruise lines' and all accessories (these usually being the
last to arrive, given the complexity of their manufacture). If there's
a particular – and particularly popular – item you were after, you're
probably already too late. You should have been there waving your
credit card a fortnight ago.

This isn't to say that there aren't still bargains to be had.
February, moving into March, also sees the designer brands launch
their warehouse sales, packed chock-full of samples (the one-off
fashion items that the brands use to take orders from the shops)
and cancelled orders (items that were manufactured but then no
longer wanted by the stores).

Meanwhile, the bigger wheels of fashion keep turning. At the
beginning of the month come the women's ready-to-wear catwalk
collections in New York, where most of the big American designers
show. The middle of the month sees the London ready-to-wear
shows, followed back-to-back by shows in Milan and then Paris.

*Modern retailers need at least eight
seasonal displays in their windows and
at least 12 ideas per season: January
sales, the first spring statements, Easter,
summer wardrobes, the summer sales,
new autumn collections, winter looks
and Christmas.*

March

Revisit stores as, increasingly, fashion brands are moving away from the classic 'two collections' a year model and, to keep you shoppers interested (and spending), now break their deliveries into four or even six collections a year. So look out in the middle of March for new pieces filtering on to the shopfloor.

This is especially true of those fast-fashion high-street retailers that specialise in reproducing (the designers may think that this is to put it kindly) designer fashions at more affordable prices: they will have new deliveries several times a week. Even the major department stores will be, across their many brands, receiving three or so deliveries a day, with up to 300 items in each delivery, so repeated visits will be worth it (like you need persuading!). Look out, too, for the increasingly popular warehouse sales – events that pull together and then heavily discount clothes from a number of well-known brands.

April/May

It's one of the mysteries of the fashion calendar (showing on the catwalks a year in advance of the clothes being in the shops is just another of fashion's timing oddities) that just as you're getting used to the nippy weather outside abating, some stores start carrying their high-summer products. It may not exactly be balmy outside, but contrary though it may be to practicality, because you probably won't be able to wear it for months to come, now is the time to buy your summer wardrobe, especially if you're uncertain whether an item will still be around later when the sunshine finally does arrive.

June/July

Somewhere in Paris and Milan, menswear shows for the following spring/summer are under way. Don't get over-excited about these though. There is a gulf between what appears on the catwalks and the more commercial items that actually get made and sold to the stores, especially when it comes to womenswear. Some items are made simply to generate column inches. And even high-fashion designers know they have to sell in order to stay in the game.

Back in the real world ... Just 183 of them on from the New Year sales. You've been counting the days. What does that mean? Yes, it's almost sales time again. Designer-warehouse sales are still going strong, hoping to relieve you of your cash before the sales proper kick in again. Those in the know (i.e. who have registered with the organisers ahead of the warehouse sales) can be invited to previews, usually one day ahead of opening to the general public. Some stores also run 'privilege lists', inviting V.I.C.s (very important customers) to preview evenings when they can buy items at sale prices ahead of the sales.

It may also be worth having a store card for some department stores too – not to load up with interest-heavy purchases you can't pay off, but in order to be invited to sales previews at which an extra discount is offered to cardholders only. Even those not on lists or holding cards can make discreet enquiries with sales staff as to the marked-down prices of items they have an eye on.

The secret to successful sales shopping is pre-planning: a recce of each store, a note of the item you may want to buy if the price is right, an enquiry as to what the price will be and turning up on the first day of the sales to nab it. By July the summer sales are in full swing for most stores, running through to the end of the month.

August

My, it's chilly outside. After all, it is the height of the British summer. Maybe that's what all the shopkeepers are thinking when they start putting chunky knitwear and heavy coats on to the racks. Yes, it's the arrival of the new season's stock. As ever, don't delay in snapping up something that really takes your fancy unless you're ready to gamble that it will still be about when the weather turns or you're confident of finding a better option when all of the deliveries have finally been made.

No matter how big the discount, a store almost never sells at a loss.

September

The new deliveries keep coming and the weather is turning, so expect sales to pick up and demand for the items you've earmarked to increase rapidly. Designer-warehouse sales kick off again, offering an alternative bargain scenario, with discounts of up to 60 per cent. The stock is unlikely to offer much in the way of current season products, but you are just as likely to pick up items as ideal for the change of weather as anything you'll find in the stores.

Over in New York, the women's ready-to-wear collections for spring/summer are showing on the catwalks, with London following in the middle of the month and Milan towards the end of the month.

October/November

The start of October sees the spring/summer collections shown to buyers and press in Paris. Back in the stores, cruise collections (between-season collections that give a foretaste of what to expect for the forthcoming spring/summer) hit the shopfloors and keep coming right up to Christmas.

Spring/summer collections proper start filtering through now, with retailers hoping to catch a few early sales with customers going somewhere warm and sunny over the Christmas holidays. By the middle of the month some designer brands will have their full collections on show – these are the pieces that, come the imminent sale time, are under an annoying sign that reads 'New Collection! Not in the sale'.

Had a busy day? Use your time more wisely. British women spend an average of eight years of their lives shopping. That's 301 trips to stores a year, 15 of them for shoes. They spend 48 hours a year just looking in the windows. Get a life!

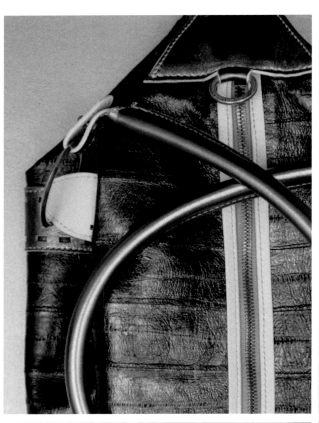

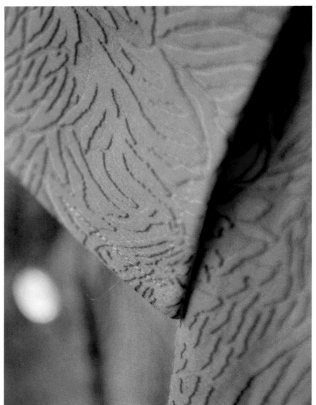
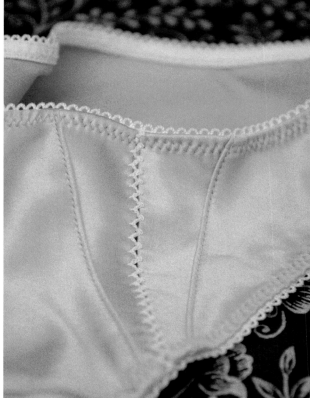

December

The new season pre-collections start arriving in the stores and will keep doing so in dribs and drabs until February, as the New Year sales are winding down. Up to 70 per cent of a buyer's seasonal budget will have been spent on these collections, so stores are banking on you to go and buy them. You are no doubt only too willing to help out in any way you can. Don't spend all your readies though: those New Year sales are coming. It used to be that store sales dates were set in stone, leading to spectacles of slightly sad people queuing around the block or even camping out overnight (it must be one hell of a deduction to make that worth while). While most sales traditionally start on Boxing Day, many retailers now keep their options open and respond to the mood of the moment. So keep your eyes – and your wallet – open.

Most stores will start with reductions of between 20 and 30 per cent (who are those stores who knock off a measly 10 per cent trying to kid?), building to around 50 per cent, with only the least in-demand stock warranting a 70 per cent deduction. Perhaps the more disturbing aspect of these figures is that no matter how big the discount, a store almost never sells at a loss. The very worst-case scenario is that it breaks even and recovers the wholesale price that it paid to the brand. Think of that next time you pay full price for something.

One final way of making a few savings that may not be ecologically sound involves planning ahead. Flights to the world's fashion capitals (Milan, Paris but especially New York) can be had for a reasonable price (although they rise drastically in the run-up to the Christmas holidays). A shopping trip to New York might get you the same designer clothes available in the UK at a third cheaper again (though remember that, over a certain expenditure, duty is payable on these items and you will need to factor in other costs before deciding whether the potential bargains are really worth their overall cost).

KNOW
BEFORE
YOU GO

OK, you now know to which fashion tribe you belong. You've learnt a few more tricks of the trade, and you know the best time to secure the best bargains. Now it's your day off, your debit and credit cards are burning a hole in your purse and you're just desperate to get to those shops.

But are you really ready to face the high street? Let's do a quick recap on a few of the things we have learnt so far.

Shopping survival

1 Don't stand for shoddy service

If you're not being served, walk out. Shopping is about so much more than a sales transaction and shops that haven't got the message yet ought to get out of the game. Even if the shop itself is twenty years past its last refurbishment, it's amazing how much we will forgive if the staff are knowledgeable and friendly and recognise us as individuals. The worst offenders of all are those who take your money while barely acknowledging your presence. Not far behind are the so-called service professionals who, when an item is out of stock, are incapable of offering you any kind of reason, consolation or, better still, a viable alternative. Getting it right is so simple. In my opinion, people who don't give a hoot about providing an exceptional customer experience ought not to be trading. While reviewing our biggest chain stores I have generally experienced poor, indifferent service. This is largely due to businesses letting loose inexperienced and unmotivated staff on the floor.

In one shop I visited for my weekly magazine column, the assistant manning the till was on the phone for the first 15 minutes I was in there – she might have been sorting out a delivery, but somehow I didn't think so as she kept referring to the number of Bacardi Breezers she'd downed the night before. One day high-street retailers will learn the hard way that the service experience is the backbone of all shopping. Frankly, I think the online retailers are better at service than bricks-and-mortar retailers. I always ask for the manager when I feel under-served. Most shop managers have the authority to look after you in one way or another and many have the possibility to give a discount.

■ *In 2005 the fashion industry produced more than £4bn worth of goods and employed over 85,000 people. Some 70 per cent of its workforce is female – with most of the rest undecided.* ■

2 Never shop on a Saturday

OK, you've got the day off, but so has the rest of Britain. I usually try to get out there mid-morning on a Wednesday or Thursday. By the afternoon the merchandise is often all out of place and the staff are flagging.

I remember my first job in retail was at Harrods' Way In. Saturday was by far our worst day. From Monday to Friday the staff were generally able to look after people well. On Saturday it often turned into a bun fight due to the sheer volume of traffic in the store. The white limos that now pull up outside its doors disgorge cackling tanned girls on hen weekends. Hideous.

3 Dress the part

If you flick through the weekly magazines you'll note that practised celebrity shoppers almost always wear flat shoes and dress down in jeans and vests to be as comfortable as possible while shopping. I can always spot what New Yorkers call the 'bridge and tunnel' brigade (which means those who've come in from out of town, dressed up in high shoes and fancy clothes) – don't shop in these clothes as they make you look as though you're trying too hard. The women tend to be the Russian-wife types who leave lippy on garments – they think the sales assistants give them scarves as an accessory. No, sweeties – it is to cover your overworked, over-made-up faces.

One more thing – go shopping on a good-hair day. It sounds daft, but if your hair looks bad, the whole outfit just won't feel right. The same applies to your make-up.

4 Go online first

Do your research online, from the comfort of your armchair.
I like to check out US *Vogue*'s www.style.com or the British site
www.vogue.co.uk after the catwalk shows to get ideas for what's
coming. I also use www.net-a-porter.com, www.matchesfashion.com
and www.brownsfashion.com to check out the season's key fashion
pieces. I also read www.wgsn.com (it's the clothing industry's
trade bible) to keep up on industry developments.

5 Don't buy in haste

Never buy rashly. If you're not sure, even for a moment, don't
buy it. If you've got the time and don't mind taking the risk, put
everything (except the most exceptional items) back until the end
of the day so you can make your final choice. As so many of the
stores sell different versions of the same thing, you can really pick
the cream of the crop. I still feel a touch of nausea whenever I open
my wardrobe and see the most ridiculously teetering pair of Terry
de Havilland gold platform shoes I bought in London's Dover Street
Market. The words 'total fashion victim' come to mind, but I do love
looking at them.

*Some 70 per cent of all supermarket
purchases are impulse buys. If we did
the same in fashion stores, we'd need
wardrobes the size of Elton John's.*

Product by product

When it comes to different product categories, there's a little specialist knowledge you need to make the right choice. Here's the lowdown.

Lingerie

There is one cardinal rule when it comes to lingerie shopping: know your size. You may think you know this already, but 75 per cent of women in the UK wear the wrong size bra (they think that they're smaller in the back and larger in the cup than they actually are, so who says it's only men who over-estimate what they've got?). Wearing the wrong size has a negative effect on comfort, the health of your breasts and your silhouette. Women are, on average, getting bigger (up from 34B to a 36C over the last decade), but because your weight fluctuates, it's important to get fitted every six months.

Nothing can ruin an outfit faster than an ill-fitting bra. This may seem unlikely – you can't see it, after all. But it will affect both your posture and the way your clothes hang. It may even lead to what they, in the bra industry, call 'double busting' – where the wiring cuts into the breast and creates a spill-over of flesh. If nothing else, it makes you look overweight when you're very possibly not.

So when we say fitted, we don't mean just measured. This entails going to a small, independent underwear store and investing some of your time – a proper fitting could take anything up to 45 minutes (it's best to go mid-morning, after new deliveries have been made to the store, or mid-afternoon, after restocking). With some stores you may need to make an appointment to be fitted.

Shop for lingerie with an open mind: price, for instance, is no indication of quality in underwear. Be ready to try on plenty of options – underwear is now as subject to fashion as any other part

of your wardrobe so don't be set in your ways. And always buy with purpose: is it for everyday work or a hot date? This will help you whittle down the huge choice. If comfort is the key issue, as it should be for everyday wear, aim for a full cut and cotton (because it's breathable). These factors are much less important with what those in the trade discreetly call 'bedroom pieces', because these aren't designed to stay on for long anyway. More and more women are thinking of underwear as an accessory to be co-ordinated with their outerwear. But it is black (along with white, the two best-selling colours) and nude that are most useful. Nude offers the best 'invisibility' under clothes – better even than white.

Remember also to buy at least two pairs of matching knickers (of whatever style) for each bra purchased. I tend to go for whatever is most comfortable (you can always pack a sexier pair and change later if the moment arises) and always think that a co-ordinated set looks better, though I have to say that I hate G-strings – they're the ugliest thing ever invented, even if they do hide VPL. Much better to choose a clearly designed and flattering pair of briefs. It doesn't, however, pay to buy bras in multiples if you find a style you love – you'll need to be refitted in six months so it is better to buy again then and wear your current stock until it turns grey.

The ideal capsule wardrobe for everyday underwear is:

- a black plunge bra (with removable padding)
- a sports bra
- a nude strapless bra
- a smooth-lined (i.e. no seams across the front of the cup) T-shirt bra, also in nude

Indeed, you'll want most bras to pass the t-shirt test – to be invisible worn under a tight T-shirt. So that's the perfect item to wear when you go shopping for underwear.

Jeans

Jeans used to be a commodity item – made by the truckload and sold (relatively) cheaply, as befitted their heritage as the stuff of workwear. You wore them until they fell apart, then you bought another pair. But the market has been revolutionised: jeans are now a fashion item, with new brands launching almost weekly. That makes shopping for jeans not only arduous and time-consuming – prepare to set aside a whole day – but also confusing. When buying jeans, it pays to look at the detail.

Take the fabric for instance. The best is made in Japan, where original looms are still made and where the selvage (the strip of white fabric along the inside of the seam, visible if you turn a leg back) is an indication of the fabric quality that more mass-market jeans will not have. This kind of 'raw' indigo denim, unwashed and untreated, will, however, shrink considerably on washing, unless washed at a very low temperature or dry-cleaned, so allow for an inch in the waist and two inches in the leg (also be careful what you try it on with – indigo dye can rub off and stain lighter-coloured clothing). On the other hand, all denim stretches with wear, so keep this in mind if buying a very fitted pair.

Other details to consider include:

- rivets (exposed, covered or absent altogether)
- fly (zip, which on tighter styles can easily break, or buttons)
- pocket details (the plainer, the more formal)

Although denim can now be bought in a multitude of different washes, it's dark, untreated denim that is most versatile – easy to dress up or down and even passing muster on many formal occasions these days, worn with a pair of sandals, for instance (though it is always better to try on jeans with flat shoes, as these will give a truer representation of your shape in the jeans). Dark denim also looks better with age, ageing in a way that even pre-distressed/aged jeans cannot convincingly mimic. They are also more slimming, especially if worn with a centre crease.

Of course, for most women the greater concern is that of fit. The most important areas to consider are the waistline, the rise (the distance between the waistband and the crotch) and the thigh (leg length can always be altered).

Unfortunately the classic pear shape that most women in the UK are means many jeans fit either on the thigh and gape around the waist, or fit on the waist and are too tight around the thigh. Some dedicated women's brands are now cutting their own cloth to avoid this problem, but for most brands it remains a question of finding a happy compromise. The pear-shaped may find that a boot-cut jean is the key style. As for 'Does my bum look big in this?', the golden rule is that the bigger your rear end, the larger the rear pockets should be. Tiny pockets will only accentuate your behind.

But you know what? My rule is that if wearing jeans doesn't make you feel great, just don't wear them. Only buy a pair of jeans if you really love them (and I have so many pairs that I thought I loved at the time but that I hardly ever wear) and if they make you feel sexy. If they don't, my advice: buy some trousers.

When buying jeans, it pays to look at the detail.

Coats

The golden rule: avoid fashion coats, unless you want to find it stuffed at the back of a wardrobe a year later having been worn, ooh, three times. Stick to the classics: a princess cut (that slightly shrunken look), a trench coat (it may not be that warm on its own, but it's what fashion types call 'trans-seasonal') or an A-line coat to help cover larger rear ends.

Unless you're exceptionally tall, length should be no longer than your knees, and remember that belted styles tend to make the wide look wider still. And make sure the colour is neutral – grey, navy, black, fawn – because it has to be worn with pretty much everything in your wardrobe. This is especially true for leather coats (one of these can be a great investment piece). Only take a leap of faith in terms of colour or style if you're buying what might be called a summer coat – a lighter, thinner layer that keeps the breeze at bay, but not a nasty cold. Personally I'd never buy a coat in a bold colour as it will just date too quickly.

When you're out shopping, dress as you would for work because this is what you'll be wearing most of the time you're also wearing your new coat. Remember, though, that there's a good chance you'll be wearing something chunky under the coat so, although the new season deliveries are the best time to buy (the spread of sizes a coat is available in shrinks rapidly), you may have to dress against the prevailing weather to make the wisest purchase. Don't go coat-shopping in a T-shirt and shorts just because it's sunny outside.

Why this safe, nay, boring approach? Because you should be thinking of getting a year, or even several years' worth of almost daily wear in the cold months from this garment. This means paying out at least £300 for an item that needs to be of a certain timeless style and quality to withstand both the wear and tear and exposure to the elements.

And once you've found your dream coat:

- Check the lining – if it is of poor quality or badly stitched it's a good sign (or rather a bad one) that the coat is not going to go the distance

- Make sure buttons are securely fastened (coat buttons undergo a lot of strain) and that the coat comes with spares

- Make sure the fabric, which ideally should be pure wool (better than a synthetic mix, even one mixed with a luxury fabric like cashmere), is a tightly woven one. A loose weave will not only catch on bag clasps and the like, but will also be less weather-resistant. Tweedy and herringbone weaves are especially hard-wearing. Coats made of professional, technical fabrics are best of all for facing bad weather, but unfortunately these tend to be sporty in style and thus not hugely versatile

And, as with any investment piece, look after your coat. Don't leave it crumpled at the bottom of the wardrobe: get it dry-cleaned regularly and when not in use for extended periods keep it wrapped in a plastic cover. That way, although it will lie forgotten and alone during the hazy days of summer, come next winter it's ready to be your reliable friend and protector again.

Dresses

I do think it's amazing how dresses have really replaced separates over the last couple of years. I remember my mother always had a couple of timeless evening dresses that came out time and time again, but it's hard to do that now.

Ignore the trends. That may seem like strange advice when it comes to buying fashion, but it holds true for dresses perhaps more than any item in your wardrobe. Why? Because a dress is not a coat. If a coat, for instance, needs to be warm and protective as well as attractive, a dress is just about looking good, feminine, sassy. And the effectiveness of a dress in doing this is not about being trendy – it's about finding a dress that best suits your body shape. So if the prevailing trend doesn't suit you, just go your own way.

Go with the basic idea that a basic dress shape best suits a basic body shape:

an Empire-line dress is good for the short

a drop waist dress good for the slender

an hourglass cut good for the curvier woman

the busty should avoid the baby doll. Unless very busty is the desired effect of course. And who are we to say it shouldn't be?

And the most versatile length for all is on or just above the knee. Anything else looks extreme and is likely to date quickly.

The time of year you're shopping for a dress is also pertinent as there is a gulf between winter and summer dresses, both in terms of their fabrics and versatility: the heavier weights of the wool or jersey winter dress, for instance, restricts its use; the lighter cottons of some summer dresses can at least be layered up for more year-round wear. Summer dresses also tend to be easier to dress up or down. In contrast, those who aren't confident about their legs might consider wearing a shorter-than-usual dress during winter when the dress can be teamed with thick tights.

Regardless of the time of year, take both heels and tights when shopping for a dress – both can transform the look of a dress.

While you're trying on, make sure you pay close attention to the zips, buttons, seams and the finishing of the hem – this is the best way to judge the quality of the dress and how long it is likely to last. Because dresses are, on the whole, fitted, there is considerably more strain on the (often thin) fabric than other garments are subjected to. If there is any strain when you're checking yourself out in the mirror, either go a size up (it's OK to do this, honest – only you'll know and the dress will look that much better on you) or don't expect it to last long enough to become a wardrobe favourite.

Similarly, if buying a more obviously glamorous dress for a special occasion, consider what extended use you may be able to get from it. If you buy a striking fashion dress with the intention of making a statement, be prepared for the extravagance of perhaps wearing it only once (people remember, even after a few drinks) and always ensure that you feel comfortable in it – occasionwear attracts attention as it is.

A more classic style, especially one of a more practical length, may be more easily dressed down and so have an extended life beyond your big occasion. It's worth being ready to spend more on the kind of dress that makes this possible: your number of 'wears per pound' will make it better value. Try on as great a variety of dresses as possible, eliminating unsuitable shapes and colours as you go. And always try on your dress at home, in your own environment, before committing to keeping it.

Men's tailoring

The good news is that, thanks to advances in cutting and manufacturing techniques, the options in good suits has never been better. If once there were a vast chasm between high-street off-the-peg and made-to-measure suit (a basic block then altered for a better fit), as there was between made-to-measure and bespoke suit (a suit made from scratch to your exact specifications), now the gap is closing.

Just follow some simple rules to buy the best and you won't go wrong:

■ Avoid synthetic fabrics

■ Buy from more traditional retailers/brands, most of which will be happy to carry out minor alterations in leg and sleeve length, thus getting round some stores' antiquated insistence on selling jacket and trousers as one item of a standard bad fit

■ Wear the kind of shoes you intend to wear with your suit when shopping

The bad news is that it still pays to make the investment, because a suit is only as good as its fit and fit is determined by the quality of cut and craftsmanship. This is especially the case given how, for the same money as a branded fashion suit, a better-fitting classic suit (unless you're unusually average in size) could be had. And classicism is really what suits are all about.

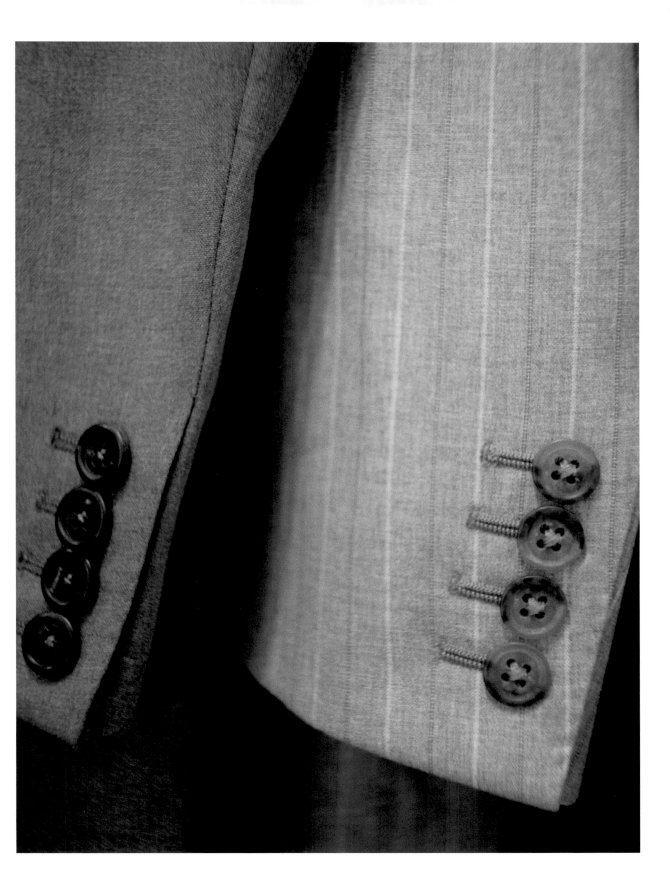

Similarly, while a bespoke suit may, on paper, seem rather expensive (though you needn't go to Savile Row – your local tailor will be proficient), the man hours it requires makes it very good value. A bespoke suit is typically made from high-grade fabrics, has some extra fabric built into it (so it can grow larger as you do) and, with care, will last decades (another reason why an expensive fashion suit can be a flash in the pan). More than this, because the bespoke suit is made just for you, it enhances all your positive traits and effectively hides the less positive ones. A bespoke suit is not for those in a hurry, however – it may require three fittings with you and could take up to three months to make.

With any suit, there are some basic style rules:

- Nothing should be exaggerated: the classic suit is fitted at the shoulder, full in the chest, gently nipped in at the waist

- The most versatile is a two-button (or three-button for something less formal), single-breasted jacket with peak or notch lapels

- Trousers should be flat fronted and gently tapered

- Black suits should be left to restaurant staff and doormen at trendy hotels. Always go for navy blue or charcoal grey, this being the blank canvas on which you can paint your personality with your choice of shirt and tie. But not too much personality – to paraphrase the 19th-century dandy Beau Brummell, who effectively invented the modern suit, 'the man who is noticed for his dress is not well-dressed at all'

Shoes

Ah, shoes ... seemingly the Achilles' heel (no pun intended) of almost every woman's shopping. You go out for a loaf of bread. You come back with shoes.

Yet despite this extensive practice, lots of women get their shoe shopping wrong. The biggest fault is a lack of honesty with oneself, especially over sizing. Yes, leather does stretch over time, but not even a half size, while stretchers and more traditional techniques (stuffing them with wet newspaper) only serve to soften the leather as your feet would otherwise do. In other words, if the shoe doesn't fit, it doesn't fit. Don't buy them.

Honesty is also required because not all shoes suit all people: sandals require nice feet, for instance; towering heels can just make some women look unstable, not elegant. And if you see something you like at the start of the season, my tip is to buy then – there's a good chance they won't be available, or not in your size, later on. I even buy my summer sandals in January – that's advanced planning!

Difficult though it is for many women (because women tend to have an emotional attachment to the shoes they see and buy, whereas men are more practicality/investment-driven) a degree of detachment is required for successful shoe shopping. This will help you approach shoes with some focus. The selection is so vast today that it is all too easy to get distracted. But some sense of whether your choice is 'fit for purpose' will at least ensure that you come away with what you need: don't come back with sparkly sandals if your intention was to buy boots for that hiking holiday; shop with a sense as to whether the shoe is for partying or working in. I buy two very distinct types of shoe with two different expectations of how they'll work for me: I have comfortable shoes for work and what I call 'car to bar' shoes that I can pose in without worrying too much that they'll kill my feet.

In fact, the key factor in any shoe-shopping decision here is style vs comfort – you may be willing to forgo comfort while socialising for a few hours, but not for days on end in an office, especially in a job in which you're on your feet a lot. Indeed, making shoes that are both stylish and comfortable – because the two are not mutually exclusive, despite the common misconception that they are – is one of the main challenges facing the footwear industry. Clarks, however, is one British brand flying the flag for this cause, and doing it rather well.

It is worth adopting that male investment thinking with work shoes – because you'll do more miles in them than you will in those sparkly numbers – and with classics. These are those shoes that are hard to get excited about, but that you know will be useful over and over again.

It is the classics that make up the essential capsule footwear wardrobe:

- the pump
- the driving moccasin
- good trainers
- mid-height sandals
- ankle or knee-high boots
- the clog
- the thong or flip-flop
  (in leather, not the plastic variety)

Need evidence that women like bags and shoes? From 2005 to 2006 sales of men's accessories grew by just 5 per cent. Sales of women's accessories grew by – ahem – 68 per cent. That's £350m worth. Men in contrast spent just £156m and half of that was ... ties. Boring!

In seeking out the right shoes (OK, are any shoes the wrong shoes?), a specialist shoe retailer is more likely to have the expert knowledge to help you with your choice, rather than the 'Which size?' bunnies who just hop between customers and the stockroom all day.

Always pay attention as to whether you are buying quality shoes:

Leather is preferable to anything synthetic – it will wear better and breathes, which is better for your feet

Look out for shoe technology – padding, shock absorbency, under-foot layers, even anti-bacterial systems, all of which are increasingly being found in even the glitziest of shoes

Check the neatness of the stitching and the balance of the heel in proportion to the rest of the shoe – does it look right?

And avoid buying any shoes that show signs of creasing – this is a result of just a handful of people trying on this style before you. So you can imagine what state they will be in after a few wears out on the town

Bags

It may be so terribly tempting just to go out and buy the latest it-bag. But hold on. For one, you're probably too late. These bags often sell out before they even make it to the shelves. If you really want one, you have to be there either soon after the new-season deliveries or, better still, butter up the staff in advance – they should be able to show you through that brand's look-book (a guide to that season's collection) and arrange for one to be put aside.

But are you sure you really want one? It's the it-bag that, insiders will tell you, typically results in the brand boosting their production at a cost to quality – the more an it-bag is in demand, the greater the number of returns. That's another reason to get in there early: the first production runs of the bag are likely to have been made with more care.

The it-bag, of course, is also the one that is likely to be counter-feited or to 'inspire' a close copy – suddenly your precious it-bag isn't so itty. It's everywhere. More than that, I think it's sad. I see someone with an it-bag and think 'Saddo – where's your individuality?' It's the worst kind of gullible label love there is.

This is one reason why even bag buyers will advise customers to buy a classic over a fashion bag. Several hundred pounds is a lot of money for something that might look naff in just a few months (if you do insist on an it-bag, be ready to use it every day – it's the only way it will ever be cost-effective). I just want a great work bag that can also look good out at night. In other words, a classic.

A classic may cost no less but it is an investment purchase, probably capable of giving a lifetime's service. Providing, that is, that you've first pondered just exactly what you want this bag for and how you may prefer to carry it – by the hand, in which case make sure it feels comfortable in the hand, or over the shoulder, in which case make sure you wear your thickest coat when shopping. Are you the kind who is ready to roll with just a purse, compact and phone? Or the kind who likes to look as though she's moving home?

Evening bags are more for display than practicality – you're buying an object to flaunt (though it does serve as a portable pocket if you're in a dress). It just has to be big enough to squeeze in credit card, lipstick and keys. The everyday bag, in contrast, has to be:

- **Tough** – choose thick leather, which will age well (though some specialist leathers, such as deer and kangaroo, can be thin and hard-wearing)

- **Sturdy** – check how secure the (preferably double) stitching is and ensure that the handle is fastened to the body of the bag in such a way that it passes all the way under the body

- **Secure** – a metal zip covering the entire opening

- **Functional** – internal pockets will help you find your keys/phone/bus-pass in less than the standard five minutes

- **Dark in colour** – or with light-coloured leathers you need to accept its inevitable grubbiness as part of its character or resign yourself to a routine of regular cleaning and protection (consider also if you're a regular wearer of indigo jeans, as the dye rubs off easily)

- **Light in weight** – a bag that is heavy when empty might suggest quality, but not usefulness

Finally, for some women it has to go with your shoes. Don't go holding your shoes up to the bag because you're unlikely to find a perfect match and because they will never be seen this close anyway. The lighting at arm and ground level is always different and that's how they should be viewed: as they'd be worn.

Jewellery

The first question is: shouldn't someone else be buying you the jewellery? The second is, what do you want jewellery for: as a fashion item? As a piece of self-congratulation? And the third is, are you prepared to hunt and keep hunting?

The options in jewellery are so vast – if you factor in vintage pieces and the selections of independent retailers, many pieces are one-offs – that the only way to find what you really want is to devote time to it and, essentially, to be ready to try on lots and lots of the stuff, even if this can be intimidating in some stores (a piece of jewellery never looks the same on as it does in the display case). This is why some research ahead of time can be invaluable – you may know you want a pink stone, for instance, but that alone could mean a diamond, ruby or crystal. When it comes to high-street jewellers, brands such as H. Samuel and Ernest Jones both have great websites – easy to navigate and comprehensive collections online, which makes shopping so much easier and accessible.

But even within one type of stone the variety is huge, which makes comparing like for like a fruitless exercise. Add in the variety of craftsmanship between pieces and there really is no such comparison. Good advice, then, is critical so try to shop at reputable jewellers. The jewellery-retail business in the UK remains a small one, so reputations are hard won and easily lost. Putting yourself in an expert's hands (rather than trying to make yourself an expert) also helps maintain some of the mystique that is central to the pleasure of jewellery.

More and more jewellery is now branded, with 'name' jewellers and jewellery designers offering distinctive pieces in a house style. Inevitably, they also charge a premium for their work and for the big-brand experience that some stores – the likes of Tiffany – offer when shopping with them. I personally always opt for a statement piece, but I find that invariably you have to pay for them: a cheap statement piece just looks cheap. And whatever jewellery you buy, it has to work with the outfit you wear it with.

But a brand goes not guarantee quality. Always:

- Examine the piece you're considering carefully: turn it over and look at the back (this is where, if the maker has cut any corners, the signs may be seen)

- Handle it – the piece should be smooth without any rough catches

- Examine the finish – are the hinges solid?

It may take a few outings to 'get your eye in', so try to avoid buying the first piece that takes your fancy. Remember that, arguably, jewellery says more about you than any other accessory.

It is also very worth checking out jewellery fairs for individual designer-makers, many of whom you'll be able to meet face-to-face here. You may even choose to have a bespoke piece made just for you by one of them – it's not as expensive an option as you might imagine and not only allows you to have some creative input but also results in a piece that is unique.

For the same reason, antique jewellery is also well worth considering because the pieces often embody a history and a level of craftsmanship hard to find in modern work. Always ask the dealer about its age, provenance and whether there have been any alterations to ensure that the piece is not an over-priced reproduction. Finally, do be prepared to spend. It may be a generalisation, but in an age when diamond rings are now sold through supermarkets, the more you spend the higher the quality of stone or level of craftsmanship you'll get. That said, the true value of any jewellery is in its intrinsic value to its wearer – and only you can bring that to the party.

Watches

There are watches and then there are watches. In the first category come fashion items, usually boldly styled, inexpensive (at least compared with what you could pay for a watch) and functional. Yes, they tell the time, but they are really an extension of jewellery. Then there are what you might call proper watches. These are almost certainly Swiss-made and probably automatic (they wind themselves through movement) and mechanical. Quartz (i.e. battery-driven) watches almost killed of the mechanical watch industry during the 1980s, but it has since made a remarkable recovery.

Why? Because mechanical watches are complex to make, requiring the skills of specialist craftsmen, and because of this they tend to represent the kind of watches sold by the major international brands, for which there is also a premium to be paid. In other words, these watches are not really about telling the time – they're about an appreciation of craftsmanship, history, mechanics and status. In other words, again, they are particularly male in their appeal.

Although this new interest has led to a thriving second-hand and part-exchange market (and it is worth checking out reputable dealers selling authenticated and serviced watches, ideally with all paperwork and the original packaging), even these are decidedly investment pieces. When someone buys a watch like this, usually it is a watch for life – some brands even position their watches as heirlooms in the making. I know from my own experience: I own a 1979 Patek Philippe that I utterly adore, the best investment I ever made and one I want to hand down to my children. When my dad died, the only material thing the family mourned was the loss of his watch (it went to his second wife). In other words, I've found that watches can be loaded with emotion. So choose carefully.

Typically it is classic styles that sell best. Diving or aviation designs (which have the added bonus of making you feel really macho) or chunkier dress watches make for the best everyday, wear-with-anything watches, while more extreme styles may look out of place on occasion. Note, however, that some of the better designs are not by the more mainstream brands – this may put off those who just want a label to flash around. And some of the most iconic watches are loaded with less desirable connotations that can be hard to shake off. Those who simply want a great watch should look further afield.

So-called 'complications' (largely pointless but mechanically advanced add-ons, such as a chronograph or moon-phase display) will increase the price. Indeed, although there is much debate among watch buffs as to which movement (i.e. the wheels and cogs that whirr inside) is best from watch to watch, to all practical intents there is little between them, though, ironically perhaps, none of them will keep time as exactly as a cheapo digital. But keeping time is not really what these are about.

Worn for years, a leather strap will need replacing, as much as every year. And if you want the one designed to go with the watch, this can mean a hefty bill. All mechanical watches should really undergo a service by the company that made them every few years, again at some cost.

Watches, in other words, are an investment both in terms of your time and your money (they may even push up your contents insurance). Take some time before you make your decision.

Some brands promote their watches as heirlooms in the making.

6

ARE YOU
BEING
SERVED?

I am seriously in awe of somebody who manages to get good service from even the most unhelpful of sales assistants.

You know the type of customer I'm talking about – they have the patter of car salesmen with all the honey-like charm of a Casanova. And, despite their gooey front being utterly transparent, it somehow always works with sales assistants. The quality of service Mr Smoothy receives is simply superior. Just how do he and his type do it?

For one thing , this type of customer is friendly, even if it is an actorly kind of friendliness. It's all too easy to get bolshy with sales assistants, in part because so many of them aren't competent, in part because the simplest question – 'Do you have this in any other colour or size?' – is often met with a dumbfounded, zombie-like emptiness. But venting anger and frustration – even that caused by something else entirely – will not help your cause.

Being communicative will, though: smile a lot and look the person you are dealing with in the eye and address them by name (if they're not wearing a name badge, tell them your name and ask theirs). It's only polite. Sales assistants aren't the automatons they might well be taken for and, in many stores, theirs can be a thankless job – dealing with demanding, moaning, rude people, so mind your Ps and Qs.

Use their name next time you visit the store (the more you visit, the more you become a 'regular', and the more success you will have in getting good service). They may not remember you at first but they'll be pleased you remembered them. Build a relationship and reap the rewards. It's much easier to handle an important issue – mysteriously, the colour of that top that suited you so well in front of the shop mirror doesn't suit you at all in front of the bedroom mirror – if you can work on a person-to-person basis, especially if that person happens to be someone who can fix your problem.

Similarly (and this is a personal bugbear), although some sales staff seemingly find it impossible to hand a card or change back to the customer, choosing instead to place it on the counter top for the customer to collect, don't stoop to their level. When paying, put your money in the sales assistant's hand. They are not diseased.

If you can talk to sales assistants and managers as you might someone at the bus stop – casually – then you can start to make suggestions. These shouldn't be confused with complaints and, if delivered in the right way, shouldn't be taken as such. But if there's something simple that annoys customers and that can be easily put right, why not point this out? You're helping them improve their business as much as your shopping experience. By the same token, don't accept the 'That's not up to me, I just work here' answer. It begs the reply, 'Then who is it up to? When can I speak to them please?'.

As in life generally, if you don't ask, you don't get. So you want a discount? What harm is there in asking? The chances are that in a chain store maybe the manager only is permitted to offer regular or high-spending customers a discount and then rarely – head office will have set certain rules. But in an independent store the prices are much more flexible.

Don't be arrogant with it, but remember that the competition is stiff out there – that blouse, or something very like it, can probably be found elsewhere. To find it may be an inconvenience, but retailers know they need to keep customers happy: studies show that the vast majority of shoppers will not return to a store if they feel it has in some way betrayed their trust or abused their 'relationship'.

Lastly, it pays to know what you are, and are not, entitled to. By this I don't mean a free glass of champagne and a selection of slaves to follow you around the store, but in the legal sense. There's a lot of bluff in retail but in fashion retail especially: perhaps because our whims are at their most changeable when it comes to clothes shopping and shopkeepers feel the need to protect themselves. Know what is your right as a fashion consumer.

How to complain

It's frankly a little embarrassing. And it's not very British. We may mutter under our breath, hold grudges and prefer to keep the useless item of clothing than have to suffer a till tirade, but complain is what you have to do if you're not getting the service that you expect.

Now, expectations can be misleading. But service should match the quality of the goods on sale and the environment in which they're sold.

We all know that designer-fashion shops can be rather sniffy, just as high-street shops can all seem to be staffed by students and part-time workers who really seem not to care less. Here's a theory: it is, unfortunately, a consequence of British history and its class system in particular that we have an innate horror of servitude. To serve someone well takes skill. It is a profession. But here, unlike in America or Italy, for example, it is not considered so. The consequences can be shoddy. And they won't get better unless people vote with their wallets, and also let the shopkeepers know.

Diplomacy is key

Making a complaint in person is much like getting good service in the first place. It requires the same mixture of wiles, charm, politeness and diplomacy. Remember that, unless you are in a small independent store, you are likely to be dealing with an employee and not the employer so they are unlikely to take anything you say about their products too personally (complaints about their service are another thing entirely).

Don't go storming in demanding to see the manager – respect (or at least assume) that the sales assistant has authority to act on the store's behalf. Be calm and to the point, remembering that it is only reasonable of you to give the store the opportunity to remedy your problem. State what you want calmly, even if you're furious (and know what you are entitled to, without quoting the book at them). It is a fine line when dealing with some people, but be assertive rather than aggressive. Take with you the faulty goods, any packaging and proof of purchase.

The management

If you meet resistance and have seemingly exhausted all options with the sales assistant, state politely that you would like to continue to seek some resolution to the situation and ask to see the manager. This may mean having the same conversation twice but you are now dealing with someone responsible for the store and, hopefully, keen to maintain good customer relations. Any complaints about individual members of staff should be directed initially only to the manager.

Take a letter, Miss Jones

If you meet a dead end with the manager, explain that you would like full contact details for the head office and the head of the company – a full name, address and phone number. The store, if its address is different from that of the head office or its trading name different from that of its parent company, is legally obliged under the Business Names Act (1985) to give you this information on request. Do not accept the address or phone number of a remote customer-complaints department.

Explain clearly that you intend to write to this named individual to pursue your complaint, mentioning, by name, that you spoke to the store manager, and that you will send a copy of the correspondence to the manager (always keep a copy for yourself too). This is not meant to sound like a threat. It is simply acting on your right to complain.

In the letter, again state details of what you bought, where and when, the price you paid, any reference number from the receipt (but not the receipt itself – never send original documents as you're quite likely never to see them again), the reason for your complaint, a reasonable deadline for their response and, crucially, what you would like to happen to resolve your claim and by when. Sometimes just stating this clearly is enough – it reassures the retailer that there is a clear way to bring a speedy end to the issue and hopefully satisfy (and perhaps keep the custom of) a customer.

As a side issue, you'll get much further if your letter or e-mail is clear and to the point, pleasant, free of insults (you are, after all, speaking to the people with the power to remedy your problem, or not) and grammatically correct. An intelligent letter gets an intelligent response (we hope). And don't send dozens of e-mails, however tempting this may be – this actually only slows down the response time.

Be prepared to follow up your letter with a phone call, in which you should refer to the letter and agree a date by which you will have been contacted on this issue. Take details of the person you are speaking to (name and position within the company) and note when the call took place and what was said. It may be getting tiresome by now. They may have worn you down. But follow up this phone call with a second letter (the same process as the first applies). Keep at it. Don't give up.

It was the skirt that done it, m'lord

In worst-case scenarios – and if this is over a piece of clothing or a pair of shoes, it really is a worst case scenario – you can go to court. It may help to get a report from an independent expert on your case (was the shoe so poorly made that it was inevitable that the heel would snap? was the dye in the fabric insufficiently fixed and just waiting to rub off over your white trousers?), though this will be at your expense and won't necessary be reimbursed if court costs are awarded in your favour. Sometimes the shop will agree to go halves on the cost of the report if both parties (that's you and the shop) can agree first to find the results binding.

I smell a rat (and it's not my faux-fur coat)

So much for the softly-softly, smile-very-nicely approach. What's the score when you have to play hardball? A recent experience had me reaching for my *Bumper Book of Law* (you may like to reach for the latest updates in consumer law in the UK via DTI/government websites) when I tried to return a pair of faulty shoes and was told by the shop assistant that I could only do so if I still had the box.

The box? Why would I still have the box? Instinctively that just seemed improbable to me. I could sense someone either trying to pull a fast one or who just didn't know what they were talking about. And I was right ...

Know your rights

Like any other consumer situation, when you buy a fashion item you enter into a kind of unspoken contract with the friendly shopkeeper. This means that, like it or not, they have obligations towards you as a shopper. The most fundamental of these are that the item they've sold you must be 'of satisfactory quality' (so it shouldn't fall apart next day and the material shouldn't be flawed). It must also be 'fit for its purpose' (so although their stratospheric height or lack of padding may stop you walking in those heels, they're not fit if the heel pokes up through the insole like a spike, or if a jacket is meant to be waterproof and isn't). And it must be 'as described' (so if it says size 10 on the ticket and you later find it's size 16, or if you're forced to shop blindfold for some reason and are told the sweater is green and when you take your blindfold off it's blue, you have a right to take action).

What's more, you're within your rights to ask for a refund, or request a replacement (assuming the item is in stock or can be ordered in), even if you've worn the item a few times. There is what is called the 'right to reject' goods that prove faulty. The law allows you adequate though unspecified time to check the item before concluding that it is, indeed, coming apart at the seams. However, your right to reject lapses if it takes you too long to examine your purchase and discover its fault. In that time you are deemed to have accepted the goods. In other words, don't delay to check out your purchase and act quickly if a fault materialises.

If the fault is minor, the shop can offer to make good the item with a repair. But if the repair is shoddy you can still then demand a refund or replacement or even money in order to get the repair done properly yourself. Better still, if the shop arranges the repair, it has to be carried out within a reasonable time (you and the shop will have to agree on what is reasonable according to circumstances) and without any inconvenience to you. And if the repair can't be done at a reasonable price, then, once again, you're entitled to a refund, though the retailer may argue for a reduction if you've obviously worn the item.

Other shops will offer you a credit note, but you don't have to accept this. If you do, remember that it can't be changed for cash later, and it may have an expiry date. By the by, all of these rights apply to items reduced in a sale as much as to full-price ones. It is against the law to display a sign saying there are 'no refunds on sale goods'. Actually, unless the sign is accompanied by a 'this does not affect your statutory rights' clause, it is against the law to display one saying just 'no refunds' too. (Technically this is, to quote from my *Bumper Book of Law*, 'an attempt by the trader to exclude liability for a breach of your statutory rights', and if you can quote that you'll really put the wind up 'em). If the goods are faulty you're entitled to a refund, end of story.

There's always some toing and froing in these situations, but the bottom line is this: if you're entitled to a refund, repair, replacement or compensation, it's the shop that has to sort out the problem. Legally they can't tell you to send it back to the manufacturer or offer to send it back for you 'for them to assess the problem', or some such buck-passing. Your relationship is with the store you bought the item from. If it turns out that the shop is buying faulty goods from the manufacturer, that's their problem.

Don't delay to check your purchases and act quickly if a fault materialises.

What to do

The first thing is to not take the mickey. There are those swindlers who buy an item, wear it to the office party and then try to return it. Don't. It's bad form. Don't create a fault that wasn't there either – fashion retailers have a good sense of where faults may appear on a garment that has had reasonable use. Be good. But if you spot a genuine fault, stop wearing the item; check that you have read the care label correctly and ensure that the fault hasn't been a consequence of your raucous partying or because you saw no harm in playing football in your pointy heels.

Next, find your proof of purchase. It's up to you to prove where and when you bought the item. The receipt is obviously best so it pays to keep all your receipts, even if it's in a box under the bed. That said, your rights still hold whether you have the receipt or not, but some proof of purchase will probably be necessary: a bank statement or cheque stub are legally valid proofs of purchase, bags and packaging from goods exclusive to that shop may count, even your friend's word, assuming they were with you when you shopped, can help.

And don't hang around: take the item, proof of purchase and any packaging you may have (but are not obliged to have kept) back to the shop in person. If you can't do that, write to them or call them, even if it is simply to notify them of the fault and your intention to visit the store at a later, more convenient date. If you call, make sure you get a full name and title for the person you speak to, and make sure they have your full name. Note the time and date.

If the item you have bought is bulky – a really, really heavy pair of boots or a complete ski wardrobe for instance – you can ask the shop to collect it for you, but not if you have 'accepted' the goods (i.e. taken your time to find out they're not suitable) and not if they were a present. Whenever you have a present that is faulty in some way it's always best, if possible, if the actual buyer returns the item in person.

Queens of clean

Yes, I'm talking to you people who think nothing of spending countless pounds on the upkeep of the fashion items you could wash and iron yourselves if you weren't so busy buying more clothes – you even have rights in relation to your dry-cleaner. Dry-cleaning, consumer law specifies, must be done 'with reasonable care and skill', 'within a reasonable time' and 'for a reasonable charge'.

It's probably the care and skill part that is most likely to land you in hot water (and maybe even your clothes). If their cleaning has been poor, or if their cleaning has made the item grubbier than it was before it went in, you should give the cleaner a chance to clean it again (at their expense). Failing that, you are entitled to a refund. The same goes for damage caused by dry-cleaning: if they can fix the problem, you should allow them to make a repair. If they can't, you should expect compensation – perhaps the cost of having it repaired elsewhere or, if the repair isn't possible, the full price that you paid for the item (though the cleaner may request a reduction for the wear and tear to the garment). Once you spot a problem, act quickly.

There remain a few caveats, however. Dry-cleaning won't get out all stains. If, while you were writing that letter of complaint, your fountain pen exploded over your cream silk blouse, don't expect miracles of your dry-cleaner. Similarly, dry-cleaning can make some stains stand out even more. It's your call whether to take the risk. If you lose your dry-cleaning ticket, that's just tough. And remember that the fault may not have been caused by the dry-cleaner but through the item's inferior manufacture. In which case, take it up with the shop where you bought the item.

One cautionary note: sweeping statements about the dry-cleaning service printed on the back of a ticket – 'no responsibility for loss or damage to garments, however caused' – are, strangely enough, not illegal. But these kinds of terms, which are get-out clauses in effect, are not enforceable if a court finds them unfair.

Paying for it all

The downside of being a fully paid-up shopper is the actual nitty-gritty of how to pay for all your splurges.

The good thing about credit cards

Most people use credit cards for one reason: to extend to themselves a little extra spending power that they might not otherwise have at that time. But there are other, better reasons for buying with a credit card as opposed to with a debit or charge card: under the Consumer Credit Act, it may extend your consumer rights. Buying on credit often means that your credit card company is equally as liable for any faulty clothes that you buy – or for a failure to deliver ones that you've ordered, or if you've been sent the wrong clothes – as the shop where you bought them or the catalogue or internet site you ordered them from.

This doesn't mean that you get double your money back. Some spoilsport closed that loophole before it even had the chance to open. But it does mean that you can contact your credit card company instead of the store if you choose. Write to the credit card company with your account details explaining the situation and be prepared to chase it up. They may then make you an offer of compensation for the faulty goods, which you can either accept or negotiate for a better deal.

There is a little small print though. The purchase needs to amount to more than £100 – that's your purchase in total in the shop (or on the internet site) in question on that occasion, not the cost of the single faulty garment. There's an upper limit of £30,000. But if you've managed to spend that amount of money on clothes in one hit, you can probably afford to go and buy another. Finally, if you're not up to date with your credit card payments, (a) don't expect much help, and (b) you really should cut back on your shopping!

Money up front

If you're really desperate for something in store but can't afford it right now, or simply can't take it away with you at that moment, or want to order something the store doesn't have in stock, you may have the option to pay a deposit.

The basic rule is to avoid paying a deposit unless you absolutely have to. If you do, check the store's terms first: is it refundable if you cancel the order or change your mind? If so, under what circumstances might the store keep the deposit? Get a receipt for your deposit, with the store's name and address on it. Pay by credit card if the deposit is over £100 (potentially this gives you extra cover). And of course make sure that the business to which you're giving your money for nothing in exchange is bona fide and likely to be around to fulfil your arrangement.

Sales of fashion online have increased by 461 per cent over the past five years – but that's still only 3 per cent of all clothing and footwear spending. So it seems we still prefer to be in shops than at our PCs. It's the youngsters – those aged 15 to 24 – who are the biggest online shoppers.

Store cards

Store cards always seem like a good idea at the time, especially given how persuasive some sales staff can be in tempting you to sign up (remember, they often receive a bonus for having done so, so their motivation is not pure). After all, you're getting money off perhaps, and it means you don't have to pay now. But, as with your rights in relation to the return of faulty goods, it pays to read the small print.

Just what is the APR (annual percentage rate) on the card? Unless you're planning to pay off the bill in full when it comes, it's this that will determine the true cost of your purchase. There may be an interest-free period, but unless you can honestly assure yourself that you will pay your bill off in full during this time, what's the interest rate afterwards? Are there penalties for not making a payment? Can you afford to take out the optional Payment Protection Insurance (PPI)? It makes your bills more expensive, but may protect you if you can't make a payment.

All in all, store cards are money traps to more people than they are help to the few who use them wisely. The temptation to sign up for one is always greater because you're typically standing amidst lots of stuff you'd really quite like, and the store card seems to make it instantly available in the way your bank manager might not. It's better not to sign on the spot – instead, take the agreement home and think about it. It's almost always better to use some other method of payment. Better than that, if you really can't afford something, don't buy it. But who are we to tell you how to manage your money?

One last tip: if you ever find yourself waiting for a shop to respond to a complaint or in dispute with a shop over, for instance, a refund for a faulty garment, don't be tempted to withhold payments on your store card in protest. This will not do you any favours.

The bad news

Fashion shopping is a fickle business. One minute you think you look a million dollars in that camisole top – usually when you're desperate to buy something, anything, it's closing time and your bored partner is saying you look great in it (NB they are past caring) – and about £1.35 the next.

Also fickle is weight: you're svelte one week, a bloater the next. So, too, is the amount of common sense Mama Nature graced each of us with.

Here are the warnings: you have no legal rights to expect anything of the shop from whence you bought what you thought was a lovely camisole if (a) it doesn't fit, (b) you change your mind, (c) you examined the clothing when you bought it and should have seen the fault, or (d) you bought the wrong item for the intended use. No, that camisole will not keep you warm on your Arctic expedition. There is also an (e) which might seem obvious, but you'd be surprised how many people try it on. No, you don't have grounds for complaint if you damaged the item yourself. Too darn bad.

Furthermore, although the clothes you buy should be free of all defects, if the sales assistant points them out to you before you buy the item – by telling you, for instance, that the item is a 'second', 'shop-soiled' or 'sold as seen' – you cannot return the item with a complaint about the defect. Often store managers will, if asked, offer a discount on a shop-soiled or slightly damaged item on the condition that the sale is 'final'; which is to say, don't try and take it back for the fault for which you received the discount. One last thing: if you return an item because it's faulty, the burden of proof is on the consumer to prove the fault was there when bought.

There is a fine line between a seam starting to come apart before you've ever worn the item and one that splits once you've worn it – one is faulty, the other is, arguably, just poorly made. But perhaps you only paid a fiver for it. If you paid considerably more and it soon starts to come apart, arguably it's not 'of satisfactory quality'.

More and more – but not all – retailers, in the spirit of competition or good customer relations, offer policies beyond your statutory rights (i.e. they may allow you to return an item within a certain time frame simply because you change your mind), so it's worth finding out what these are on a shop-by-shop basis before you buy.

The boot on the other foot, fashion shopkeepers will also tell you of the problem of goodwill being abused by customer expectation: the customer who comes in and says, 'I bought these pants three years ago and after boil-washing every week since, I'm disappointed to find that they're looking rather tired.' Clothes wear out. Get used to that idea. In fact, rejoice in it. It's one more excuse to go shopping.

Caveat emptor

It's an old Roman expression and it means, in effect, 'let the buyer beware'. It's good advice if you're buying fashion items from anywhere other than a legitimate source: so, not a temporary market stall (bona fide market stalls require a trader's licence that is often displayed), a man and his suitcase, a car-boot sale, the bloke down the pub – count all these as illegitimate sources.

The fashion industry (and its offshoot, the fashion-brand fragrance industry) is rife with counterfeits. Counterfeits deny the manufacturer the profit on the design, development and marketing that made the item so desirable in the first place. Some may discount this money as being a drop in the ocean to such big companies, but in sum such profits are often important in keeping that company or its sub-contractors going. Morally, they are as much the company's right as profit from the sale of stock belongs to the store that sells it. That means buying known counterfeits is ethically no better than buying stolen goods or shoplifting. Counterfeit fashion is also a known source of laundering money for the drugs, terrorism and illegal arms trades. Finally, there is the question of self-delusion: if you know the item is fake, who are you really trying to kid when you wear or carry it? You are a sucker for branding – because you have certainly not bought into quality if you've bought a counterfeit.

Lecture over. Back to your rights: you have none. If you think you have found a genuine bargain, be cautious. Pay close attention to the quality of the goods, labelling and packaging you're intending to buy – but these days fakes are so accurate even this probably won't tell you much. Ask if there are any guarantees – chances are there won't be. And, finally, be very suspicious of too-good-to-be-true prices. A £500 bag being sold for £50 is not an unwanted present. It is not surplus or dead stock. It is not a second. It is almost certainly a fake.

It is a criminal offence for a trader of any description to say something untrue about the goods – for example, this is a such-and-such designer bag when it's been made in a faraway sweatshop. Not that this law will do you much good, especially if no alarm bells ring when the seller insists on being paid in cash. When he disappears into the twilight, the internet auction site closes overnight or the seller's e-mail address ceases to be recognised, there is no recourse. You've lost your money. And your dignity.

Private chancer

The same warning applies to the purchase of goods through a private sale, such as through a private ad in the paper. The goods must be 'as described' – if the coat is meant to be made of leather and it's PVC, that's not 'as described'. And technically you can take legal action if you bought the clothing on the basis of something the seller said that proves to be false. But that's not easy to prove without a witness (who you could take along during the exchange) or with a written description of the goods (which you can request but won't necessarily get). Look out too for traders posing as private sellers.

Shopping online

Dealing with real people when returning clothes has its own pitfalls. Dealing with a faceless machine can be a more painful process altogether, with its own rules, regulations and warnings. As more clothes buying is done online, it pays to listen up. This is a complex business.

Going, going ...

Warning! Buying by internet auction is trickier still, because you have very few rights indeed. You are buying from, effectively, a private seller. Their ability repeatedly to sell from that site may be hampered by systems that allow them to be rated by past customers (many of which ratings are faked by the seller), but that won't leave the seller with the must-have bag on offer short of customers. Test the water first: does the seller have a returns policy? Where are they based? How will you get the goods? And at what cost will delivery be made? Get what evidence you can of the item's authenticity. As you would with proper, real shops, shop around with the virtual ones. Get some recommendations.

Similarly, some websites offer anti-fraud guarantees, but they are subject to myriad terms and conditions. Besides which, the internet sites' obligations to you in this instance are severely limited. They are matchmakers between buyer and seller, and nothing more.

Your rights online

With any kind of home shopping, including established internet retailers (not those, such as eBay, who merely provide an entrée to a private seller), your rights are much the same as those when dealing with a bricks-and-mortar shop. In fact, because you're giving money to a faceless operation, you are also entitled to:

(a) written confirmation or perhaps an e-mail of the items you have bought (you should keep a hard copy of this, along with a hard copy of your order and of any subsequent correspondence).

(b) a period for you to change your mind and cancel the order for any reason for a full refund – usually seven working days after the day on which you received your purchase (unless clothes are made to order or personalised, in which case there's no 'cool down' period).

(c) a full refund if the clothes you've bought are not delivered by the date agreed (or within 30 days, whichever is sooner). If you arrange to return the clothes, however, the cost of doing so falls to you.

Safety first

With any internet transaction, never give PIN numbers or account-access information; check statements after the purchase to ensure the right deduction was made and no others; note the internet site's details (an address and landline number should be included); only give details necessary to make the transaction; avoid sending cheques or money orders; use a credit card where possible; only use sites with secure, encrypted payment pages, or insist on using a dedicated, recognised payment system such as PayPal (www.paypal.com/uk). Most well-established sites use such a system.

Only ever enter personal or financial information once you know the site is a secure one: look for a privacy statement (good internet

shops all have them) and for the web address to begin with https://
(indicating a secure connection with the website). There is some
good news: if your credit or debit card details are used fraudulently,
your card issuer must arrange for you to re-credited in full.

In a bidding war, be aware that, just as in real life, when the
hammer falls you're legally obliged to pay up if yours is the highest
bid (no matter how rash) when the auction closes.

The English abroad

Finally, remember that when you're out shopping, unless you've
had a really heavy night, you usually know what country you're in
and thus what your consumer rights are under UK law. But if you
are shopping abroad or buying from internet sites that are based
abroad (and 'uk' somewhere in the website's address is no
guarantee that it is actually in the UK), the rules change.

UK law may cover your internet transaction and UK law usually
applies unless the contract (if there is one) states otherwise. You
may even have some rights under UK law even if it doesn't. That's
the theory at least. The Government's consumer advice department
warns that in practice it is unlikely you will get money out of a
company based abroad. It may be enough to threaten legal action,
but don't even think about pursuing it: the costs will be prohibitive
and the money better spent on, well, more clothes.

Buying from companies abroad also entails additional costs:
packing, shipping, currency-conversion charges, VAT and customs
duty (which varies from country to country but which is currently
at around 15 per cent for clothing from the US – see the Revenue &
Customs website for details, www.hmrc.gov.uk). These can add
considerably to your initially modest purchase. These extra costs
aren't always explicit on the internet site. It's no fun when the
FedEx man rings your bell and you sprint to the door, only to
be greeted with your package and a bill to pay before he'll hand
it over.

SHOP
STORIES

Handmade and Found

True boutiques, in the original sense of the word, were different from other shops in the way they combined personal service with a confident way of selling practically anything the owner chose to sell.

Barbara Hulanicki was the original boutique owner who inspired thousands of copycats when she opened her Biba boutique in London, most famously on Kensington High Street in 1969.

When husband-and-wife team Ruth Llewellyn and Anthony Wilson met at college in Brighton, they had much the same dream. They set up their shop, Comfort & Joy, on Essex Road, just off the main drag in London's Islington – now an upmarket shopping destination. He sourced the product and she, a trained designer, made up frocks behind the curtain. Unfortunately, their dream didn't quite match Hulanicki's. When I visited them in autumn 2006, I found a sad, little shop that was mirrored by the state of their relationship. The two had divorced some time ago but, unable to afford to lease premises of their own, they had literally divided the shop in two, with his stock on one side, her creations on the other. Think of the Berlin Wall and here you have the fashion version, without the mines or machine guns. Running a business in this way was the stuff of sitcoms. And the frostiness of their relationship was met by the frostiness of my reception: Ruth found the whole process excruciating. Anthony was blunter still: 'You make some good points and then you have some more fun and I just want to tell you to …'! And the rest of that sentence is unprintable.

I hated the name from the start. Locals told me that it sounded like a washing powder. Stranger still, Ruth told me that it was

inspired by a sex manual! Either way, it had nothing to do with fashion – indeed, comfort is often considered the polar opposite of what fashion is about, suggesting someone who has given up on style in favour of cosy slippers. The atmosphere was neither comfortable nor joyous either.

So that was the first thing that just had to go. In the spirit of what the two proprietors were about, we renamed the store Handmade and Found, a reflection of the unique or rare items that the shop sold. It was also a punchier name and an indication of a new lease of life. It also continued to reflect the division that, sadly, the two of them had suffered in their personal lives together. They even had two tills and bickered over when to open and close the store. This was perhaps their key problem: personal issues had given way to a lack of heart that had spilled over into their professional lives. They needed a boost as much as the shop did.

The buzzer entry system – something I can't stand, even on the posher Bond Street stores – had to go. We also glossed up the shop-front, from a coldly uninviting black-and-white sign to a warm pink one that stood out against rather grey surroundings. Inside, too, would require a makeover: while I visited I tried on a great top, but sadly the lighting in the changing room was … well, there wasn't any, which hardly encouraged me to buy. The whole store had the feel of a charity shop – thrown together, drab and unexciting, a reflection of the owners' loss of passion. No wonder stock wasn't moving.

I wanted to give them back the energy that had originally created the business which, if well looked after, could compete easily with the larger and more confident stores just two minutes' walk up the road, especially as it had the potential to corner the locality's population of slightly theatrical types wanting distinctive clothes without the designer price tag. These clothes were aggressively priced, but seemed to be asking a lot for the environment in which they were sold. The latter had to be brought up to match the standards of the former.

It would take more than this superficial overhaul to put Handmade and Found back on the map though. With the choice on the high street so huge, together with the squeeze on rents, independent stores have to offer something really special just to survive. As Ruth put it, 'The way the big retailers pick up on ideas and produce them in such numbers and undercut retailers like me, you have to really start to wonder if there is a place for someone like me in the high street.' The shop was scraping a profit, but had just experienced its worst ever trading year. Ruth and Anthony were pulling in just £10,000 profit each – a tough salary to live on in London, if not anywhere in the UK these days.

Their location was also a major disadvantage – close to, but yet just too far away from the trendy main drag of Islington. And, what is more, in a parade of shops that included a hardware store and a taxidermist. Clearly, they weren't benefiting from the area's local boutique culture so they would have to make themselves more of a destination store, meaning they had to be extra special. We looked around and saw that other stores were managing to pull the punters away from Islington's centre – their business represented a real opportunity to appeal to the same customers, as well as catch the neighbourhood's gradual gentrification.

But what made Handmade and Found potentially very special were the people: Ruth and Anthony. As the business was principally run by the two of them, I wanted to give them clearer roles which allowed them to be brilliant in their own areas. Certainly Anthony has a great eye for the products he sources on regular trips to the Far East and Ruth has a particular design style that has a regular following among the local luvvies. It was just that these talents were being lost amid inconsistent and unappealing presentation. The two of them had always hoped to 'put their own ideas [about style] out into the world and hope there was someone else out there that would like it', as Anthony put it. What was needed was something to get that spirit of individualism back.

Through pushing the pair to their limits, getting a promotional story into a fashion glossy, and experiencing how to dress windows at Harvey Nichols, the two of them have now rediscovered their inner creativity, the very driving force that encouraged them to open their own shop in the first place. I love the fact that, even at sales time, when most stores are at their least inspiring, these two express themselves through what I can only describe as bonkers window displays.

The fun is back in the business, and their original customers are slowly being joined by new ones discovering a shop they always knew was there but had never been tempted to enter. If you're in the area, go and visit. Pull back Ruth's curtain, catch her at the sewing machine and say hello from me!

Handmade and Found
109 Essex Road | Islington | London | N1 2SL
Tel: 020 7359 3898

One One Seven

I nearly fainted when I arrived at Diana Lazarris' gigantic shop on Banstead High Street in Surrey.

Every nook and cranny had been crammed full of clothes. If presentation is a key aspect of successful retail – and it is – this looked to be where the problems behind her shop One One Seven lay. Because Diana Lazarris was unsure as to just who her customer was, she was trying to cater to anyone who might walk through the shop door, stuffing her shop full of clothes so that it felt more like a showroom than a fashion store.

Actually, she had a very good idea who her customer was. It just happened to be the wrong idea. That would explain the mother-of-the-bride suits next to what I perhaps harshly called care-in-the-community slippers and some hideous pink dressing gowns that she had bought in because there was a hospital up the road and, as she explained, 'people do need dressing gowns when they go into hospital'. The slippers were displayed next to some really quite stylish boots – the appeal of which was entirely lost because of what they sat next to.

Her lack of understanding of who her modern customer was would also explain what she called 'the dog-walking coat', which looked more as though it would be worn by a market trader before it was likely to be worn by one of her wealthy Surrey locals. Her philosophy was, as she put it, 'to have choice'. She was spending £170,000 per annum on her stock. The wrong stock. No wonder it wasn't moving. No wonder she was making an annual loss of £82,000. 'Every time we close up I'm amazed how little we've taken,' she said. 'If no one is coming in, what's the point of being here?'

To make matters worse, because she was cramming so much into the shop, she was having to resort to desperate ways of displaying it. So many items were hung on jam-packed rails side on, it was practically impossible to see what was on offer. Much of it was still

in the protective wrapping supplied by the manufacturers, as if she were scared of customers handling the goods. And it was over-priced for the experience offered to customers by the shop.

The windows told a similarly sad story. Diana's most vital marketing tool was a wreath of plastic flowers, reminiscent of a 1970s funeral parlour. They had to go. She was not happy about this. 'I still like my flowers!' she exclaimed. We were to have many of these kinds of ups and downs while getting her shop back on track. I think at times she privately regretted letting me get my hands on it, but I believe that by the end she was in agreement with the changes I proposed and had discovered a new confidence.

I made some fairly sweeping changes too. About 50 per cent of the stock was returned, never to be reordered. This created more focus, more space and the opportunity for better merchandising. I put the right products in the window for the time of year: the coats we put in sold out on the evening of the shop's reopening. I took Diana on some more personal journeys too. She went to fashion photo shoots with *Woman and Home* magazine which taught her the basics of styling outfits, that would help both with her window displays and in making suggestions to her customers. And I even gave Diana a makeover herself – a new look that resulted in increased confidence in her abilities as a shopkeeper and style leader.

And that was the most fundamental change of all: making Diana aware that, in this area, she was in a position to offer her customers real direction in what they should be buying. She had to come to understand that her store's location represented a huge opportunity: a large shop in an area populated by older, wealthy women with busy social lives who liked a bit of sophisticated glamour and would welcome the opportunity to buy stylish clothes locally if that saved them a trip into the big city. This would, however, entail a new understanding of just who her customer was. Diana believed she was aiming at the 40-plus market. The truth is that her products were more for the 60-plus lady. One older customer told me that she didn't shop there herself, but her mother loved it. That said it all. What Diana Lazarris needed to understand was the idea that, in today's youth-saturated world, 40, 50 and 60 year olds want to stay 40 for ever, unlike their grannies who embraced ageing as a status symbol to be respected. To reinforce this, I took Diana to meet buyers at Nicole Farhi who taught her what the generation of customer she was selling to really like to wear these days.

When thinking of my classic rules of retail marketing – product and price, place and promotion – here was a shop with lots of the wrong product, priced as if the store were a luxury boutique, poorly promoted by a team desperately lacking the core skills of a fashion-retail business. The final P, 'people', is of course the most essential to retail: in this case not the person who ran One One Seven, but her understanding of the people who might want to shop there. I hope that Diana Lazarris keeps her promise to me and stays true to the rules I set down for her at One One Seven. If she does, she has the makings of a solid and profitable business.

One One Seven
161–165 High Street | Banstead | Surrey SM7 2NT
Tel: 01737 371417

Seen

It was a miserable February morning in Doncaster when I first met Kath Taylor and her partner, Jock, at their 2500-square foot boutique, Homeboy.

Kath had been selling fashion labels in the town for almost twenty years but her all-consuming passion had progressively turned to despair as a healthy profit had turned to a loss, leading her to remortgage her home. And despair had turned to desperation as the recently completed Frenchgate Centre had, in their eyes, dragged any remaining life out of their previously busy street and into the centrally heated comfort of the neighbouring shopping mall.

Homeboy started life as a genuinely innovative menswear boutique, bringing new labels to the town. As the business grew, so did their confidence and the pair launched a women's business with a similar vision. When I arrived they had lost sight of the ultimate rule of retail: know your tribe. There is a market for great independent boutiques in Doncaster servicing the fashion-following, label-loving crowd, but you have to get the right labels and talk to them in their own language.

Kath and Jock had a large store with a passionate team, but a naff and dated name, a tired environment, an odd mix of labels and poor awareness of today's fashion tribes. What was most worrying was their acute lack of financial planning. Running a shop, with the added expense of stock and staff, can be a killer. You've really got to be selling the product at a decent mark-up to secure a profit. At Homeboy, they simply weren't making enough money with each customer transaction. It was a vicious circle – the more panicked they got, the more they marked down the stock. Ouch.

Go back to Chapter 2 and you'll see that talking to the 'Saturday Nighter', and to some extent the 'Label Lover', is all about reassuring them they're wearing the right choice of brands when out with their

mates. Their bibles are the celebrity-fashion mags – who's wearing what, where they're going and who they went home with. Try to be too clever and you risk missing your market all together.

I decided to give the shop a whole new spirit on a budget. We rechristened the new shop 'Seen' – as in, if it's been seen in a magazine, on a catwalk or out on someone whose style you love, then we'll have it. I wanted to make the shop famous as an authority on fashion trends and a destination for the latest looks and how to get them. I wanted to give the store a point of view, great shopability and, most importantly, make the product look great. After some emergency budget surgery to get the shop looking as funky as the brands they were selling, and a few scraps with Kath and Jock, we reopened in early spring.

Seen is what great fashion-boutique retailing is all about – passionate people selling handpicked labels in a fun, spirited environment that they create themselves.

If properly nurtured, the new look Seen should get the pair back on the map of fashion retailing in the north of England. A little like an afternoon in Topshop on Oxford Circus, a trip to Seen should give the local tribes the fashion buzz they crave and keep them coming back. Together we created a big promise. I just hope they have the energy and creativity to live up to it.

Seen

18 Scot Lane | Doncaster | South Yorkshire DN1 1ES
Tel: 01302 812112

ju-ju

I had a real problem with ju-ju. While Brighton's famous North Laines, bristling with bohemian boutiques, are wonderful to stroll through, there aren't a whole lot of people spending money there on fashion. And what clothes shops there are, are mainly selling cheap T-shirts to the local students.

ju-ju became something of a local landmark when it opened 13 years ago, with its trademark zebra-striped exterior, characterful owners Soly and Tim, bubble-gum machine and quirky voodoo artefacts. When I first visited ju-ju, it just felt horribly dated and cluttered and quite frankly irrelevant. And sadly Soly and Tim came over as rudderless and lacking any form of enthusiasm. A collection of horrible, vulgar children's T-shirts felt like their last-ditch attempt to salvage things. My initial reaction was of having come across a shop that simply wasn't worth saving.

Then I spotted the remnants of a spark in Soly. Here was a girl who had once been a bit of a rebel. Back in the 90s, it was her passion for original style and fashion that had led to her opening the shop in the first instance, selling secondhand alternative labels (which nowadays we call vintage). I talked to her about a shopping tribe I call the fashion rebels. Think Amy Winehouse and Kelly Osbourne and you've got it – individual rock-chic types who dress in an utterly individual way.

I hoped she could talk to the fashion rebels in a language they would understand. I hoped that together we could create a new,

not-to-be-missed fashion destination in Brighton and that our ideas could rekindle in Soly a passion she had clearly lost somewhere along the way.

My approach was to bring in a selection of up-and-coming designers, photographers and film artists and ask them all to make contributions to the overall product and look of the store. There are a lot of arty types to be found on this stretch of the south coast and the Laines have the kind of creative buzz you get when wandering around the streets of San Francisco. I designed a mad window display to complement the striking and eye-catching exterior of the shop and brought in a bespoke Converse shoe design service. I also gave Soly a mini makeover and generally taught her to understand how to make her new, revitalised store a mecca for individual cool hunters and fashion rebels in the Brighton area.

ju-ju
24 Gloucester Road | Brighton | East Sussex BN1 4AQ
Tel: 01273 673161

Directory

Many of the shops listed in this directory have branches nationwide – in these cases we've listed the flagship store and given their website to help you find a branch local to you.

DEPARTMENT STORES

Debenhams
334-348 Oxford Street, London W1C 1JG
(0844 561 6161/www.debenhams.com)
If you can get through the clutter and people, there are some good designer bargains.

House of Fraser
318 Oxford Street, London W1C 1HF
(0870 160 7258/
www.houseoffraser.co.uk)
Don't expect a riveting shopping experience but you will get good service and some very good labels.

Fenwick
63 New Bond Street, London W1A 3BS
(020 7629 9161/www.fenwick.co.uk)
I love the ease of shopping in this store as it always has what I want and is never overcrowded. A real old fashioned gem on nouveau New Bond Street.

Harrods
87-135 Brompton Road, London SW1X 7XL (020 7730 1234/www.harrods.com)
Don't go on a Saturday. Don't go in a sad hired limo. Head straight for the women's fashion as it's the best floor in the store.

Harvey Nichols
109-125 Knightsbridge, London SW1X 7RJ (020 7235 5000/
www.harveynichols.com)
Start in the 5th floor bar and work your way down. Make sure you take in the windows on your way in. Still the best in the world.

John Lewis
278-306 Oxford Street, London W1A 1EX
(020 7629 7711/www.johnlewis.co.uk)
Don't expect to be seduced and inspired. Do expect to find what you want at a good price served brilliantly.

Liberty
Regent Street, London W1B 5AH
(020 7734 1234/www.liberty.co.uk)
A visual tactile feast.

Marks and Spencer
458 Oxford Street, London W1C 1AP (020 7935 7954/www.marksandspencer.co.uk)
Amazing food department with fashion getting better.

Peter Jones
Sloane Square, London SW1W 8EL
(020 7730 3434/www.peterjones.co.uk)

The more upbeat and fabulous arm of the good old John Lewis partnership.

Selfridges
400 Oxford Street, London W1A 1AB
(0870 837 7377/www.selfridges.com)
The place to go if you are looking for a super-sensory, madly fast-paced shopping experience.

HIGH-STREET FASHION

All Saints
57-59 Long Acre, London WC2E 9HL
(020 7836 0801/www.allsaints.co.uk)
Young, streetwear-inspired clothing chain.

Coast
12 St Christopher's Place, London W1U 1NQ
(020 7486 0911/www.coast-stores.co.uk)
Classy collection for young women, strong on dresses and suits.

COS
222 Regent Street, London W1B 5BD
(020 7478 0400/www.cosstores.com)
H&M's more sophisticated sibling is a useful new resource for elegant basics.

Crew Clothing
36 Duke of York Square, London SW3 4LY
(020 7730 7820/
www.crewclothing.co.uk)
Essential weekend wear and must-have accessories – both men's and women's wear collections.

Diesel
130 New Bond Street, London W1S 2TB
(020 7520 7799/www.diesel.com)
Slick London flagship of sexy Italian denim brand.

French Connection
396 Oxford Street, London W1C 7JX (020 7629 7766/www.frenchconnection.com)
Good-quality, irreverent fashion label fuses catwalk looks with sassy attitude.

Fullcircle
13-15 Floral Street, London WC2E 9DH
(020 7395 9420/www.fullcircleuk.com)
Cool, contemporary clothes for men and women.

Gap
376-384 Oxford Street, London W1C 1JY
(020 7408 4500/www.gap.com)
Great classic basics with amazing service and a fresh American smile.

H&M
261-271 Regent Street, London W1B 2ES
(020 7493 4004/www.hm.com)
Amazing fashion finds if you don't mind tripping over the stock on the floor.

Hobbs
84-88 King's road, London SW3 4TZ

(020 7581 2914/www.hobbs.co.uk)
Classic womenswear. Good for safe knitwear, tailored suits and well-made shoes.

Jacques Vert
Department stores nationwide (0191 521 3888/www.jacques-vert.co.uk)
An excellent array of exquisitely detailed matching shoes and accessories, offering the opportunity to shop for the 'total outfit'.

Jigsaw
126-127 New Bond Street, London W1S 1DZ (020 7491 4484/
www.jigsaw-online.com)
Tasteful womenswear known for age-spanning styles and good-quality natural fabrics.

Karen Millen
247 Regent Street, London W1B 2EW
(020 7629 1901/www.karenmillen.com)
For grown women who still want to be sexy chicks.

Lacoste
223 Regent Street, London W1B 2EQ
(020 7491 8968/www.lacoste.com)
Classic and still modern.

Mango
235 Oxford Street, London W1R 1AE
(020 7354 3505/www.mango.com)
The latest trends, tempered with laid-back Spanish style, at low prices.

Massimo Dutti
156 Regent Street, London W1B 5LB
(020 7851 1280/www.massimodutti.com)
This Zara stablemate delivers luxury looks for men and women at high-street prices.

Mexx
112-115 Long Acre, London WC2E 9NT
(020 7836 9661/www.mexx.com)
Fashion-conscious Dutch brand outfits the whole family, from baby gear to workwear.

Miss Selfridge
214 Oxford Street, London W1W 8LG
(020 7927 0214/www.missselfridge.co.uk)
Everything for hip young chicks, including specially selected vintage.

Miss Sixty
31 Great Marlborough Street, London W1V 1HA (020 7434 3060/
www.misssixty.com)
Cheeky Italian denim and separates.

Muji
135 Long Acre, London WC2E 9AD
(020 7379 0820/www.muji.co.uk)
The Japanese lifestyle store offers a range of well-made, good-value basics for men and women in muted colours – especially T-shirts and underwear.

New Look
500-502 Oxford Street, London W1C 2HW
(020 7290 7860/www.newlook.co.uk)
Breathtakingly cheap interpretations of
the latest trends for young women and men.

Oasis
12-14 Argyll Street, London W1F 7NT
(020 7434 1799/www.oasis-stores.com)
Classy young and sexy high-street brand
covering all the current trends.

Planet
Department stores nationwide
(01915 213888/www.planet.co.uk)
Planet's strong tailoring heritage provides
contemporary fashion to the modern
professional woman.

Principles
260 Regent Street, London W1B 3AG
(020 7287 3365/www.principles.co.uk)
For dressed-up ladies forty plus.

Reiss
Kent House, 14-17 Market Place, London
W1H 7AJ (020 7637 9112/
www.reiss.co.uk)
This aspirational high-street chain turns
out slick, designer-lookalike clothes for
both sexes.

River Island
301-309 Oxford Street, London W1C 2DN
(0844 395 1011/www.riverisland.com)
For every twentysomething who lives for
the weekend.

Topshop
214 Oxford Street, London W1N 9DF
(0845 121 4519/www.topshop.com)
This ground-breaking emporium of cheap
chic offers everything from designer
capsule ranges to vintage clothing and
pocket-money priced catwalk-copy
accessories.

Warehouse
19-21 Argyll Street, London W1F 7TR
(020 7437 7101/www.warehouse.co.uk)
The full gamut of trends with mid-range
pricetags.

Whistles
12 St Christopher's Place, London W1M
5HB (020 7487 4484/www.whistles.co.uk)
Mid-to-upper-range label is known for its
quality tailoring, vintage-inspired styles
and lots of detail such as embroidery and
striking patterns.

Windsmoor
Department stores nationwide
(01915 213888/www.windsmoor/co.uk)
A strong heritage spanning 70 years has
built Windsmoor's exclusive foundation
of elegance and timeless styling.

Zara
333 Oxford Street, London W1C 2HY
(020 7518 1550/www.zara.com)
A phenomenon of classic, well-priced,
designer-style high-street fashion.

DESIGNER MENSWEAR

A Butcher of Distinction
11 Dray Walk, Old Truman Brewery,
London E1 6QL (020 7770 6111/
www.butcherofdistinction.com)
Unpretentious, updated classics
from British and US labels in trendy
Shoreditch. Great for tailored shirts and
jackets with a hip twist, and jeans.

Duffer of St George
29 Shorts Gardens, London WC2H 9AP
(020 7379 4660/
www.thedufferofstgeorge.com)
Famous for contemporary preppy
essentials like stripy polo shirts and
hooded sweatshirts.

Gant
107 New Bond Street, London W1S 1ED
(020 7629 3313/www.gant.com)
Outdoorsy American preppy brand.

Hackett
137-138 Sloane Street, London SW1X
9AY (020 7730 3331/www.hackett.co.uk)
Classic, quintessentially English kit
including smart suits, rugby shirts and
crewneck sweaters.

The Library
268 BromptonRoad, London SW3 2AS
(020 7589 6569)
Slick designer menswear by the likes of
Alexander McQueen and Kris Van Assche.

dunhill
50 Jermyn Street, London SW1Y 6DL
(0845 458 0779/www.dunhill.com)
The London address for immaculate
British tailoring, super-smart watches
and leather goods.

Microzine
3-4 Little Portland Street, London
W1W 7JB (020 7636 8969/
www.microzine.co.uk)
A compendium of fashion, furnishings,
books and gadgets for the aspirational
men's mag reader. There's also a store
in Liverpool.

Nigel Hall
18 Floral Street, London WC2H 9DS
(020 7379 3600/
www.nigelhallmenswear.co.uk)
Elegant modern tailoring and knitwear.

Santos & Mowen
10 Earlham Street, London WC2H 9LN

(020 7836 4365)
Premier streetwear emporium stocks
Dsquared, Patrizia Pepe and Junk de Luxe.

Sefton
196 Upper Street, London N1 1RQ
(020 7226 7076)
A good mix of stock from big names like
Comme des Garçons, McQueen and John
Smedley, plus quirky accessories.

Ermenegildo Zegna
37-38 New Bond Street, London W1S 2RU
(0207 518 2700/www.zegna.com)
The very best in Italian tailoring.

DESIGNER WOMENSWEAR

Aimé
32 Ledbury Road, London W11 2AB
(020 7221 7070/www.aimelondon.com)
A patch of Paris in Notting Hill, this
boutique sells clothes with a certain 'je ne
c'est quoi' by Isabel Marant and APC, as
well as home accessories, toiletries and
scented candles.

A La Mode
10 Symons Street, London SW3 2TJ
(020 7730 7180)
Come here for an edited selection of
illustrious catwalk collections from
Lanvin, Rochas and Marni.

Alberta Ferretti
205-206 Sloane Street, London SW1X
9QX (020 7235 2349/www.aeffe.com)
Fluid, feminine frocks in wispy fabrics are
the signature of this Italian designer.

Anna
126 Regent's Park Road, London NW1 8XL
(020 7483 0411/www.shopatanna.co.uk)
A favourite with the Primrose Hill A-list for
its unaffected combination of mid-priced
Euro and classic British lines (Malene
Birger, Saltwater, Margaret Howell),
plus its own cashmere range. There are
branches in Norfolk, Essex and Suffolk.

Aquaint
18 Conduit Street, London W1S 2XN
(020 7499 9658)
Owner/designer Ashley Isham's
sophisticated boutique showcases his
glamorous evening dresses alongside
other exclusive labels.

Austique
330 King's Road, London SW3 5UR (020
7376 3663/www.austique.co.uk)
Lovely, girly boutique showcases designs
from down-under as well as up-and-coming
London and US labels. Flirty, feminine
dresses, the latest cult denim labels and
delicate lingerie are specialities.

Celine
160 New Bond Street, London W1S 2UE
(020 7297 4999/www.celine.com)
*There's been a recent revival in interest
in the smart structured bags from this
French fashion house.*

Chanel
278–280 Brompton Road, London SW3
2AB (020 7581 8620/www.chanel.com)
*Karl Lagerfeld's reworked tweeds and the
iconic handbags are still as fashionable
as ever.*

Chloé
152–153 Sloane Street, London SW1X
9BX (020 7823 5348/www.chloe.com)
*1960s-influenced shift dresses, bow
blouses and the covetable bags and shoes.*

Christian Dior
31 Sloane Street, London SW1X 9NR
(020 7245 1300/www.dior.com)
*Super-luxe feminine fashion and flashy
accessories.*

Cochinechine
74 Heath Street, London NW3 1DN
(020 7435 9377/www.cochinechine.com)
*A hand-picked selection of labels from
America and Europe including
Sharon Wauchob, 3.1 Phillip Lim and
Rachel Roy, plus a treasure trove of cult
accessories.*

Coco Ribbon
21 Kensington Park Road, London W11 2EU
(020 7229 4904/www.cocoribbon.com)
*This girly boutique has spawned imitators
across the country: glam clothes, lingerie,
gifts, toiletries, books and homewares are
sold in a laid-back boudoir setting.*

Comptoir des Cotonniers
235 Westbourne Grove, London
W11 2SE (020 7792 9580/
www.comptoirdescotonniers.com)
*Simple, stylish fashions for mothers
and daughters.*

The Cross
141 Portland Road, London W11 4LR
(020 7727 6760/www.thecrossshop.co.uk)
*A favourite with local celebs and yummy
mummies, this unpretentious boutique
has toys and cool kids' clothes at ground
level and an eclectic range of womenswear
downstairs by the likes of Temperley,
Gharani Strok and Jenny Dyer.*

Day Birger et Mikkelsen
133A Sloane Street, London SW1X 9AX
(020 7730 9663/www.day.dk)
*Reasonably priced Danish collection
features striking prints and finishes such
as beading and embroidery.*

Diane von Furstenberg
83 Ledbury Road, London W11 2AG
(020 7221 1120/www.dvflondon.com)
*A showcase for one of the key labels of the
moment - come here for that perfect all-
purpose dress.*

Donna Karan
19 New Bond Street, London W1S 2RD
(020 7495 3100/www.donnakaran.com)
*The woman who invented the capsule
wardrobe specialises in elegant,
minimalist designs, as well as her
funky urban DKNY diffusion.*

Diverse
286 & 294 Upper Street, London N1 2TU
(020 7359 8877/www.diverseclothing.com)
*Big-league labels for men (number 286)
and women (294). The selection is
constantly changing, but expect items
by Chloé, Marc by Marc Jacobs and Day
Birger et Mikkelsen.*

Feathers
42 Hans Crescent, London SW1 0LZ
(020 7589 5802)
*A wonderful hodgepodge of pieces hand-
picked by buyer/owner Suzanne Burstein.
Maurizio Pecoraro, Rick Owens and
Humanoid are just a few examples of the
stock. Accessories are a strength, including
best-selling boots by Gianni Barbato.*

Ghost
14 Hinde Street, London W1U 3BG
(020 7486 0239/www.ghost.co.uk)
*These vintage-inspired crepe dresses
have enduring popularity.*

Jezebell
59 Blandford Street, London W1U 7HP
(020 7935 7109/www.jezebell.co.uk).
*Established and lesser-known labels rub
shoulders at this stylish shop run by a
former stylist and fashion PR - clothes are
courtesy of Vivienne Westwood, Phillip Lim
and Richard Nicoll and there are fabulous
shoes by Rupert Sanderson and Georgina
Goodman, a smattering of vintage and
lingerie, and cult jewellery from New York.*

JW Beeton
48–50 Ledbury Road, London W11 2AJ
(020 7229 8874)
*Perennially popular Notting Hill boutique
stocks a constantly changing line-up of
casual, affordable European brands, such
as Rützou from Denmark, and Transit
from Italy.*

Jesiré
28 James Street, London WC2E 8PA
(020 7420 4450/www.jesire.net)
Young, fashion-conscious label - its

*vintage-inspired dresses are especially
popular.*

KJ's Laundry
74 Marylebone Lane, London W1U 2PW
(020 7486 7855/www.kjslaundry.com)
*Young, feminine yet unfussy designs,
from London and further afield, are the
mainstay of this friendly little boutique -
star attraction are the versatile slip
dresses by Australian Lee Mathews.*

Koh Samui
65–67 Monmouth Street, London
WC2H 9DG (020 7240 4280/
www.kohsamui.co.uk)
*One of London's best-loved fashion shops.
A mix of major designer names (Marc
Jacobs, Chloé), emerging labels and
vintage mingle on the rails. There's a
dazzling selection of unusual jewellery
by young designers from around the globe,
plus the latest 'it' bags and shoes.*

Labour of Love
193 Upper Street, London N1 1RQ (020
7354 9333/www.labour-of-love.co.uk)
*An exquisite little space uniting cool
clothes with handmade accessories and
a selection of CDs and books that capture
the vibe.*

Matthew Williamson
28 Bruton Street, London W1J 6QH (020
7629 6200/www.matthewwilliamson.com)
*Bright, eye-catching colours and patterns
and youthful styles characterise this
celeb fave.*

MaxMara
19–21 Old Bond Street, London
W1S 4PU (020 7499 7902)
*Known for its well-cut classic coats and
suits, this Italian label recently gained
attention on the catwalk for more
youthful looks.*

Miu Miu
123 New Bond Street, London W1S 1EJ
(020 7409 0900/www.miumiu.com)
Prada's funky younger sister.

Mimi
309 King's Road, London SW3 5EP (020
7349 9699/www.mimilondon.co.uk)
*The emphasis is on pretty partywear
and premium denim at the Chelsea girl
about town's fave boutique - labels
include Collette Dinnigan, Temperley
and Rebecca Taylor.*

Moschino
28–29 Conduit Street, London W1S 2YB
(020 7318 0555/www.aeffe.com)
*Designer clothes with witty, sometimes
surreal, twists.*

Musa
31 Holland Street, London W8 4NA
(020 7937 6282/www.musalondon.co.uk)
A tiny gem tucked down a picturesque Kensington street combines ultra-feminine frocks with vintage pieces, lingerie and unique jewellery.

Net-a-porter
www.net-a-porter.com
The hottest designer clothes online, plus fashion features to inspire you.

Orla Kiely
31 Monmouth Street, London WC2H 9DD
(020 7240 4022/www.orlakiely.com)
The Irish designer's Covent Garden flagship sells clothing, bags, furniture and home accessories featuring her appealingly simple, signature prints.

Press
3 Erskine Road, London NW3 3AJ (020 7449 0081)
Melanie Press's chic boutique stocks cult labels including Vanessa Bruno, PPQ, Biba and 18th Amendment denim.

Ronit Zilkha
34 Brook Street, London W1K 5DN (020 7499 3707/www.ronitzilkha.com)
Elegant, classic designs are given a twist with interesting fabrics and trims.

Saltwater
98 Marylebone Lane, London W1U 2QB
(020 7935 3336/www.saltwater.net)
Vintage-inspired frocks and separates by a designer who hails from Cornwall and creates all the pretty house prints.

Sixty 6
66 Marylebone High Street, London W1U 5JF (020 7224 6066)
Rather than follow the latest trends, this bijou boutique has its own signature, eclectic style. A wide variety of unusual items, from designers such as Ashish, Sara Berman and Ally Capellino are packed into the small space.

Somi
Fenwicks, Bond Street, Koh Samui, House of Fraser, and independents nationwide (0208 810 8100)
Contemporary womenswear with beautiful embellishment and a hint of boho chic.

Souvenir
53 Brewer Street, London W1F 9UY (020 7287 8708/www.souvenirboutique.co.uk)
A clutch of Soho boutiques stocks big catwalk and avant-garde collections. Head to Brewer Street for Hussein Chalayan, Vivienne Westwood and Viktor & Rolf, or Lexington Street for younger, more casual Jessica Ogden and APC. There's a good choice of designer accessories and quirky jewellery at both stores.

Stella McCartney
30 Bruton Street, London W1J 6LG (020 7518 3100/www.stellamccartney.com)
The designer's complete collection, from sexy tailoring to bags and cruelty-free shoes.

Temperley
6–10 Colville Mews, Lonsdale Road, London W11 2DA (020 7229 7957/www.temperleylondon.com)
The designer's feminine party dresses have a devoted socialite and celeb following.

The World According To…
4 Brewer Street, London W1F 0SB (020 7437 1259/www.theworldaccordingto.co.uk)
On the edge of Soho's red light district, this long-standing subterranean store sells hip urban designs from Eley Kishimoto, Martin Margiela and Sonia by Sonia Rykiel.

DESIGNER FASHION: MEN AND WOMEN

Agnès b
35–36 Floral Street, London WC2E 9DJ (020 7379 1992/www.agnesb.com)
Stylish takes on French classics, such as floral frocks, slimline trousers and neat little coats.

Antoni & Alison
43 Rosebery Avenue, London EC1R 4SH (020 7833 2141/www.antoniandalison.co.uk)
Best known for their attention-grabbing, arty slogan T-shirts, the duo also design skirts, knitwear and accessories.

Alexander McQueen
4–5 Old Bond Street, London W1S 4PD (020 7355 0088/www.alexandermcqueen.com)
Sharp suits for both sexes and extravagant evening gowns at the former enfant terrible's flagship.

Antipodium
5A Carlisle Street, London W1D 3BH (020 7287 3841/www.antipodium.com)
As its name suggests, this is the place to come for designs from emerging talent from down-under – the style is funky and casual.

b store
24A Savile Row, London W1S 3PR (020 7734 6846/www.bstorelondon.com)
Eccentric, cutting-edge looks are the stock-in-trade here, from the likes of Peter Jensen and Bernhard Willhelm as well as more recent St Martin's graduates. B store's Buddhahood footwear plays on traditional styles.

Bamford & Sons
The Old Bank, 31 Sloane Square, London SW1W 8GA (020 7881 8010/www.bamfordandsons.com)
Luxurious classics for men, women and boys, including an 'eco' range using organic cotton. Great for basics in high-quality fabrics, aspirational accessories such as restored vintage watches and classy leather goods.

Bottega Veneta
33 Sloane Street, London SW1X 9NR (020 7838 9394/www.bottegaveneta.com)
The woven bags were the stars in the early noughties, but the classy clothes have now come under the fashion spotlight.

Browns
23–27 South Molton Street, London W1K 5RD (020 7514 0000/www.brownsfashion.com)
The grande dame of London boutiques, several interlinked shops showcase around 100 designers including Chloé, Dries Van Noten, Balenciaga, Jil Sander, and current fashion wonder boy Christopher Kane. There's a designer shoe salon, a two-floor menswear section featuring Dior Homme, Lanvin and Marni. Browns Focus across the street has younger labels and denim.

Cricket
10 Cavern Walks, Mathew Street, Liverpool L2 6RE (0151 227 4645/www.cricketliverpool.co.uk)
The WAGs' favourite boutique for designer labels in Liverpool.

The Dispensary
200 Kensington Park Road, London W11 1NR (020 7727 8797)
A longstanding hit for relaxed urbanwear.

Dolce & Gabbana
6–8 Old Bond Street, London W1S 4PH (020 7659 9000/www.dolcegabbana.it)
The Italian duo's sex-saturated collections, including the famous corset dresses, are still going strong.

Dover Street Market
17–18 Dover Street, London W1S 4LT (020 7518 0680/www.doverstreetmarket.com)
Comme des Garçons' London boutique is laid out like a 'market' on six floors, featuring other loftly labels such as Alaïa, Lanvin and Pierre Hardy in displays that look like art installations.

Egg
36 Kinnerton Street, London SW1X 8ES
(020 7235 9315)
*A wonderful shop hidden in a
Knightsbridge mews selling unique
garments ungoverned by the whims of
fashion, yet undeniably stylish. Owner
Maureen Doherty used to work with
Issey Miyake, which accounts for the
minimalist Japanese-inspired feel.*

Emilio Pucci
170 Sloane Street, London SW1X 9QG
(020 7201 8171/www.emiliopucci.com)
*The 60-year-old label's signature, swirly
psychedelic prints are splashed over
scarves, handbags, dresses and more.*

Etro
14 Old Bond Street, London W1X 3DB
(020 7495 5767/www.etro.it)
*Italian fashion house known for its eclectic,
exuberant prints (especially paisley).*

Fendi
20-22 Sloane Street, SW1X 9NE
(020 7838 6280/www.fendi.com)
*It may not be creating the fashion frenzy it
did with the baguettea few years back, but
Fendi is still a byword for fabulously funky
luxury bags and accessories.*

Giorgio Armani
37 Sloane Street, London SW1X 9LP
(020 7235 6232/www.giorgioarmani.com)
The king of understated tailoring.

Gucci
18 Sloane Street, London SW1X 9NE
(020 7235 6707/www.gucci.com)
*Known for its finely crafted shoes and
bags, Gucci is adopting a more refined,
less flashy style for its ready-to-wear
collection under its new young creative
director.*

Hugo Boss
35-38 Sloane Square, The Willett
Building, London SW1W 8AQ
(02072591240/www.hugoboss.com)
*Several collections cover everything
from slick, urban tailoring to modern
sportswear for both sexes.*

Issey Miyake
52 Conduit Street, London W1S 2YX
(020 7851 4620/www.isseymiyake.com)
*A true original, Miyake's collections,
including Pleats Please and the dramatic
main line, don't kow-tow to current trends.*

Jean Paul Gaultier Boutique
171-175 Draycott Avenue, London SW3
3AJ (020 7584 4648/www.jpgaultier.com)
*Once the enfant terrible of French fashion,
JPG still has plenty of rock'n'roll attitude.*

Kenzo
70 Sloane Avenue, SW3 3DD
(020 7225 1960/www.kenzo.com)
*Designer known for ethnic influences and
mix of colourful patterns.*

Holland & Holland
31-33 Bruton Street, London
W1J 6HH (020 7499 4411/
www.hollandandholland.com)
*Bespoke gunmaker now has a line of luxury
casual clothing for men and women.*

Joseph
77 Fulham Road, London SW3 6RE
(020 7823 9500/www.joseph.co.uk)
*Designer Joseph Ettedgui is no longer
at the helm, but the winning formula of
flattering trousers, luxurious knitwear
and sumptuous sheepskins lives on. The
flagship also sells other designer labels
and accessories. Menswear is down
the road at 74 Sloane Avenue.*

Louis Vuitton
190-192 Sloane Street, London SW1X
9QX (020 7201 4190/www.vuitton.com)
A world-class luxury retailer.

Maison Martin Margiela
1-9 Bruton Place, London W1J 6NE
(020 7629 2682/
www.maisonmartinmargiela.net)
*Belgian designer known for desconstructed,
minimalist clothes and recycled garments.*

Matches
60-64 Ledbury Road, London
W11 2AJ (020 7221 0255/
www.matchesfashion.com)
*Deluxe labels for men and women (Prada,
Marc Jacobs, et al). Matches Spy acrosss
the street focuses on independent
designers, diffusion lines and denim.*

Marni
26 Sloane Street, London SW1X 9NE
(020 7245 9520/www.marni.com)
*A cult favourite for its minimalist shapes
and abstract patterns.*

Nanette Lepore
206 Westbourne Grove, London W11 2RH
(020 7221 8889/www.nanettelepore.com)
*American designer much loved in her
homeland for her ladylike retro sensibility
and eye-popping colours.*

Paul & Joe
39-41 Ledbury Road, London W11 2AA
(020 7243 5510/www.paulandjoe.com)
*Slightly nostalgic French label with
a penchant for subtle patterns and
delicate fabrics.*

Paul Smith
Westbourne House, 120 & 122 Kensington

Park Road, London W11 2EP (020 7727
3553/www.paulsmith.co.uk)
*The king of British classic-with-a-twist
design. Sir Paul's four-floor Notting Hill
flagship unites all his collections for men,
women, children and accessories (many
featuring his unmistakeable rainbow
stripes) under one roof.*

Prada
16-18 Old Bond Street, London W1X 3DA
(020 7647 5000/www.prada.com)
*Synonymous with sophisticated,
impeccably crafted bags, shoes and
clothing.*

Start
59 Rivington Street, London EC2A 3BN
(020 7739 3636/www.start-london.com)
*Philip Start (the founder of Woodhouse)
and his wife Brix Smith (the guitarist
from the Fall) launched this pair of shops.
Number 59 stocks designer menswear and
denim plus made-to-measure suits and
shirts from its own Rivington Street label.
The glamorous womenswear shop at
42-44 sells a good choice of hot designer
labels and jeans, plus cult cosmetics
and unique jewellery.*

Ted Baker
9-10 Floral Street, London WC2E 9HW
(020 7836 7808/www.tedbaker.co.uk)
*He started as a shirtmaker in Glasgow,
but Ted Baker has come a long way since
1987. Collections include patterned shirts
and practical suits for the boys, slinky tops
and dresses for the girls, plus kids'
clothes, accessories and fragrances.*

Urban Outfitters
200 Oxford Street, London W1D 1NU (020
7907 0800/www.urbanoutfitters.co.uk)
*A host of urban designer labels is on offer
at this lifestyle emporium, including
Erotokritos, Sonia by Sonia Rykiel and
John Smedley, plus denim and vintage.*

Vivienne Westwood
44 Conduit Street, London W1S 2YL (020
7439 1109/www.viviennewestwood.com)
*The undisputed queen of radical designer
style since the 70s, Vivienne Westwood
is still going strong with her flattering,
corseted creations. The flagship houses
the Gold Label main line, Red Label and
Anglomania diffusion lines, menswear
and accessories.*

Yohji Yamamoto
14-15 Conduit Street, London
W1S 2XJ (020 7491 4129/
www.yohjiyamamoto.co.jp)
As well as his deconstructed tailoring,

the Japanese designer created the cool
Y-3 sportswear range for Adidas.

Yves Saint Laurent
33 Old Bond Street, London W1X 4HH
(020 7493 1800/www.ysl.com)
*Ultra-glam, grown-up clothes and
fabulous shoes.*

CLASSIC

Amanda Wakeley
80 Fulham Road, London SW3 6HR (020
7590 9105/www.amandawakeley.com)
*The designer is known for her streamlined,
glamorous evening dresses.*

Aquascutum
100 Regent Street, London W1B 5SR
(020 7675 8200/www.aquascutum.co.uk)
*This traditional British brand has been
given a makeover by new CEO Kim Winser
– its main line and catwalk line both pay
tribute to its heritage with takes on classic
style, including its famous macs.*

Ballantyne
303 Westbourne Grove, W11 2QA
(020 7792 2563/www.ballantyne.it)
*The original diamond-patterned
cashmere sweaters have been reinvented
in rich modern hues.*

Betty Jackson
311 Brompton Road, London SW3 2DY
(020 7589 7884/www.bettyjackson.com)
*Veteran British designer specialises in
wearable, gently tailored dresses and suits.*

Brora
344 King's Road, London SW3 5UR
(020 7352 3697/www.brora.co.uk)
*Scottish cashmere, in stylish contemporary
styles, at reasonable prices.*

Burberry
21-23 New Bond Street, London W1S 2RE
(020 7968 0000/www.burberry.com)
*The exclusive Burberry Prorsum
collection, designed by Christopher Bailey,
is firmly in the catwalk elite, and the
iconic trenchcoats are still the epitome of
timeless British cool.*

Gieves & Hawkes
1 Savile Row, London W1S 3JR (020
7434 2001/www.gievesandhawkes.com)
*As well as a bespoke service, this Savile
Row tailor has a suave, urban-edged
ready-to-wear collection, Gieves.*

Hermès
179 Sloane Street, SW1X 9QP
(020 7823 1014/www.hermes.com)
*You may not be able to bag a Birkin there
are other models sans waiting lists, plus
iconic scarves.*

Jaeger
200-206 Regent Street, London W1R 6BN
(020 7979 1100/www.jaeger.co.uk)
*Renowned for its knitwear, neat office
suits and coats, Jaeger now has a young,
catwalk inspired label, Jaeger London.*

John Smedley
24 Brook Street, London W1K 5DG
(020 7495 2222/www.johnsmedley.com)
*A byword for understated, fine merino
wool knitwear.*

Margaret Howell
34 Wigmore Street, London W1U 2RS (020
7009 9009/www.margarethowell.co.uk)
*Margaret Howell's British essentials –
crisp shirts, relaxed tailoring and classic
knitwear for men and women – pull off the
trick of being both nostalgic and utterly
contemporary.*

Mulberry
41-42 New Bond Street, London W1S 2RY
(020 7491 3900/www.mulberry.com)
*The sturdy bags have attained cult status,
but the elegant clothes, especially its leather
and suede jackets, are worth a look too.*

Nicole Farhi
158 New Bond Street, London W1S 2UB
(020 7499 8368/www.nicolefarhi.com)
*A stalwart of the British design scene,
Nicole Farhi's signatures include
oversized knitwear, loose linens, floaty
tea dresses and well-tailored suits.*

Pink
85 Jermyn Street, London SW1Y 6JD
(020 7930 6364/ www.thomaspink.co.uk)
Impeccable shirts for men and women.

Pringle of Scotland
112 New Bond Street, London
W1S 1DP (020 7297 4580/
www.pringlescotland.com)
*The heritage cashmere label just gets
trendier under ex-Gucci designer Clare
Waight Keller, with a sophisticated main
line and the younger, more casual Red Label.*

Ralph Lauren
1 New Bond Street, London W1S 3RL
(020 7535 4600/www.polo.com)
Classic American style.

NON-STANDARD SIZES

Ann Harvey
266 Oxford Street, London W1N 9DC
(020 7408 1131)
Classic styles in sizes 16-28.

Base
55 Monmouth Street, London WC2H 9DG
(020 7240 8914/www.base-fashions.co.uk)
European designer clothing in sizes 16-28.

Evans
538-540 Oxford Street, London W1C 1LS
(020 7499 0434/www.evans.ltd.uk)
*Current looks in sizes 16-32, plus petite
(5ft 3in and under) and tall (5ft 10in
and above) ranges.*

High & Mighty
145-147 Edgware Road, London W2 2HR
(020 7723 8754/
www.highandmighty.co.uk)
*Casual clothes and suits for men over
6ft 2in.*

Long Tall Sally
21-25 Chiltern Street, London W1U 7PH
(020 7487 3370/www.longtallsally.com)
*Fashionable clothes for women 5ft 9in
and over.*

Marina Rinaldi
39 Old Bond Street, London W1S 4QP
(020 7629 4454)
*Sophisticated, designerwear for up to size
28 from this arm of the MaxMara group.*

Precis Petite
Department stores nationwide
(01915213888/ www.precis.co.uk)
*Perfectly proportioned garments for the
5ft 3in and under woman, Precis Petite
offers a complete wardrobe of chic tailored
and casual clothes in sizes 8-18.*

VINTAGE

Absolute Vintage
15 Hanbury Street, London E1 6QR (020
7247 3883/www.absolutevintage.co.uk)
*Vast vintage warehouse especially strong
on accessories – choose from more 1,000
pairs of shoes arranged by colour.*

Annie's Vintage Clothes
12 Camden Passage, London N1 8ED
(020 7359 0796)
*Immaculate 1930s bias-cut gowns and
1920s flapper dresses.*

Appleby
95 Westbourne Park Villas, London
W2 5ED (020 7229 7772/
www.applebyvintage.com)
*Carefully selected designer pieces,
including Pucci and Ossie Clark.*

Bang Bang
21 Goodge Street, London W1T 2PJ
(020 7631 4191)
*Retro resale shop packed with everything
from interesting high street items to mint-
condition designer bags.*

Beyond Retro
112 Cheshire Street, London E2 6EJ
(020 7613 3636/www.beyondretro.com)
Around 10,000 items are on the rails in

this hangar-like East End space – some of it startlingly cheap, but not all of it in good condition.

Blackout II
51 Endell Street, London WC2H 9AJ (020 7240 5006/www.blackout2.com)
Clothing from the 1920s to the 1980s for both men and women, including a fab selection of accessories, hats and shoes.

Butler & Wilson
189 Fulham Road, London SW3 6JN (020 7352 8255/www.butlerandwilson.co.uk)
Known for its reproduction costume jewellery, Butler & Wilson has a stash of genuine 1920s dresses, antique bags and shawls upstairs.

Circa Vintage Clothes
8 Fulham High Street, London SW6 3LQ (020 7736 5038/www.circavintage.com)
An elegant little vintage boutique showcasing a spectacular collection of dresses from the 1920s to the 70s.

The Girl Can't Help It
Alfie's Antique Market, 13–25 Church Street, London NW8 8DT (020 7724 8984/www.thegirlcanhelpit.com)
Hollywood-style gowns, 1950s Mexican skirts, Hawaiian shirts, vintage bar accessories and lashings of leopardprint at this kitsch corner of Alfie's.

Mary Moore
5 Clarendon Cross, London W11 4AP (020 7229 5678/www.marymoorevintage.com)
This small shop showcases the personally amassed collection of the daughter of sculptor Henry Moore.

Old Hat
66 Fulham High Street, London SW6 3LQ (020 7610 6558)
Second-hand Savile Row suits go for a song, plus overcoats, morning suits and gents' accessories.

One
30 Ledbury Road, London W11 2AB (020 7221 5300/www.onlyone.com)
Unique pieces created from customised vintage items, plus vintage couture by the likes of Chanel and Valentino.

Rellik
8 Golborne Road, London W10 5NW (020 8962 0089/www.relliklondon.co.uk)
This fashionista's favourite concentrates on dramatic pieces by big names such as Vivienne Westwood and Ossie Clark.

Rokit
42 Shelton Street, London WC2 9HZ (020 7836 6547/www.rokit.co.uk)
Rokit's four second-hand emporiums stock everything from denim and leather jackets to 1950s frocks.

Shikasuki
67 Gloucester Avenue, London NW1 8LD (020 7722 4442/www.shikasuki.com)
Striking patterned dresses from various eras and a superior selection of unusual handbags are displayed in clean, white boutique surroundings.

Steinberg & Tolkien
193 King's Road, London SW3 5EB (020 7376 3660)
Probably London's best-known vintage store, Steinberg & Tolkien is packed to the rafters, so you'll have to rummage to root out treasures by Pucci or Ossie Clark.

Vintage Modes
Grays Antique Markets, 1–7 Davies Mews, London W1K 5AB (020 7409 400/www.vintagemodes.co.uk)
A wide variety of stock, from the 19th-century to the 80s in this four-dealer enclave – the array of costume jewellery is dazzling.

Virginia
98 Portland Road, London W11 4LQ (020 7727 9908)
Immaculately preserved pieces from the Victorian era to 1940s – but don't expect bargains here.

LINGERIE & SWIMWEAR

Agent Provocateur
6 Broadwick Street, London W1V 1FH (020 7439 0229/www.agentprovocateur.com)
Bright contrasting colours, beautiful fabrics and retro pin-up-girl designs have made this ever-expanding chain a global success.

Calvin Klein
65 New Bond Street, London W1F 1RN (020 7495 2916/www.ck.com)
Chic basics for men and women.

Figleaves
(www.figleaves.com)
Exhaustive online lingerie shop.

Gossard
(01525 859 760/www.gossard.com)
Since 1901 a heritage lingerie brand offering great style, comfort and fit.

Heidi Klein
174 Westbourne Grove, London W11 2RW (020 7243 5665/www.heidiklein.com)
A great range of chic swimwear and cover-ups sold all year round, plus pre-holiday beauty treatments, such as waxing and tanning, on site.

La Perla
163 Sloane Street, London SW1X 9QB (020 7245 0527/www.laperla.com)
The crème de la crème of designer lingerie.

La Senza
162 Oxford Street, London W1D 1NG (020 7580 3559/www.lasenza.co.uk)
Affordable, stylish undies and nightwear.

Myla
74 Duke of York Square, King's Road, London SW3 4LY (020 7730 0700/www.myla.com)
Appealing to women's sensibilities rather than most men's, this tasteful lingerie is subtly sexy rather than raunchy.

Rigby & Peller
22A Conduit Street, London W1S 2XT (020 7491 2200/www.rigbyandpeller.com)
Correct fitting is the priority at the Queen's corsetier, which stocks upscale brands such as La Perla and Aubade, as well as its own label and made-to-measure corsets (at the Knightsbridge branch).

SHOES

Aldo
3–7 Neal Street, London WC2H 9PU (020 7836 7692/www.aldoshoes.com)
Huge range of inexpensive, trendy styles.

Bally
116 New Bond Street, London W1S 1EN (020 7491 7062/www.bally.com)
Sophisticated, high-quality footwear.

Christian Louboutin
23 Motcomb Street, London SW1X 8LB (020 7245 6510/www.christianlouboutin.fr)
Glamorous red-soled creations from the French designer.

Clarks
476 Oxford Street, London W1C 1LD (020 7629 9609/www.clarks.co.uk)
Great value, superbly made shoes for men, women and kids, including the original Desert Boot. Still the best on the high street.

Faith
192–194 Oxford Street, London W1A 1DG (020 7580 9561/www.faith.co.uk)
Cheap takes on catwalk looks.

French Sole
6 Ellis Street, London SW1X 9AL (020 7730 3771/www.frenchsole.com)
Ballet pumps in every conceivable style, pattern and colour.

Gina
189 Sloane Street, London SW1X 9QR (020 7235 2932/www.ginashoes.com)
Dazzling diamanté evening sandals are the speciality.

Iris
124 Draycott Avenue, London SW3 3AH
(020 7584 1252)
Designer shoes by Choé, Mark Jacobs et al.

Jimmy Choo
32 Sloane Street, London SW1X 9NR
(020 7823 1051/www.jimmychoo.com)
Sleek, sophisticated shoes with the emphasis on elegant high heels.

Kurt Geiger
65 South Molton Street, London W1K 5SU
(020 7758 8020/www.kurtgeiger.com)
Great-value interpretations of current catwalk looks as well as more classic shoes for men and women.

LK Bennett
130 Long Acre, London WC2E 9AA
(020 7379 1710/www.lkbennett.com)
Ladylike updated classics.

Office
57 Neal Street, London WC2H 4NP
(020 7379 1896/www.office.co.uk)
An eclectic selection of footwear for the young and trendy, plus a wide range of cool trainers.

Lollipop London
114 Islington High Street, London N1 8EG
(020 7226 4005/www.lollipoplondon.com)
A hand-picked selection of less-exposed British and European designer shoes is displayed in this chic little Islington boutique.

Manolo Blahnik
49-51 Old Church Street, London
SW3 5BS (020 7352 3863)
The king of sexy high heels has been at this address since the early 1970s. Prices are high, but the craftsmanship and creativity of the designs are worth it.

Pied à Terre
19 South Molton Street, London W1K 5QX
(020 7629 1362/www.piedaterre.com)
Mid-priced collection fills the gap between high street and designer.

Poste Mistress
61-63 Monmouth Street, London
WC2H 9EP (020 7379 4040/
www.officeholdings.co.uk)
The designer sister of Office sells its own reasonably priced range plus shoes by British and European designers.

Russell & Bromley
24-25 New Bond Street, London
W1S 2PS (020 7629 6903/
www.russellandbromley.co.uk)
A mix of well-made classic and fashion-forward styles appeals to a broad age range and tastes.

Rupert Sanderson
33 Bruton Place, London W1J 6NP (0870
750 9181/www.rupertsanderson.co.uk)
Elegant, British designed, Italian made shoes in classic shapes and sometimes unexpectedly flashy colours.

Shellys
266-270 Regent Street, London W1B 3AH
(020 7287 0939/www.shellys.co.uk)
Inexpensive fashion-led footwear.

Stuart Weitzman
Harrods, Selfridges and Russell & Bromley
nationwide (0207 629 6903/
www.stuartweitzman.com)
Stuart Weitzman is one of the most recognised shoe designers in the world. He offers a wide range of styling from casual to evening and he is renowned for his creative use of unique materials in footwear and for attention to fit.

Tod's
35-36 Sloane Street, London SW1X 9LP
(020 7235 1321/www.tods.com)
Best-known for its studded driving shoes, this Italian label has branched out into fashion-forward styles and bags.

ACCESSORIES

Accessorize
22 The Market, Covent Garden, London
WC2H 8HB (020 7240 2107/
www.accessorize.co.uk)
Wide range of affordable accessories in a rainbow of colours.

Anya Hindmarch
15-17 Pont Street, London
SW1X 9EH (020 7838 9177/
www.anyahindmarch.com)
Hindmarch designs sleek leather handbags as well as her popular Be A Bag service enabling customers to have their own photo printed on a variety of styles from washbags to roomy totes.

Asprey
167 New Bond Street, London W1S 4AR
(020 7493 6767/www.asprey.com)
Luxurious jewellery, china, crystal, fragrance, clothing and leather goods.

Bailey of Hollywood
Stocked in indepedents nationwide
(01946 818 275/www.baileyhats.com)
One of the world's leading hatters established 1922, this American headwear company remains a favourite with the Hollywood elite.

Bill Amberg
21-22 Chepstow Corner, London W2 4XE
(020 7727 3560/www.billamberg.com)

A wide range of well-crafted leather goods spans briefcases, stylish handbags, luggage, desk accessories, even shooting bags and sheepskin baby carriers.

Coccinelle
13 Duke of York Square, King's Road,
London SW3 4LY (020 7730 7657/
www.coccinelle.com)
Mid-priced Italian leather bags.

Connolly
41 Conduit Street, London W1S 2YQ
(020 7439 2510/www.connolly.co.uk)
Upmarket driving accessories – leather-bound atlases, espresso machines you plug into the car lighter – and timelessly chic clothing and leather jackets for men and women.

Elliot Rhodes
79 Long Acre, London WC2E 9NG
(020 7379 8544/www.elliotrhodes.com)
The humble belt is elevated to a fashion item, with hundreds of straps and buckles on display for you to create your perfect combination.

J&M Davidson
42 Ledbury Road, London W11 2AB (020
7313 9532/www.jandmdavidson.com)
Beautifully crafted retro-inspired bags, plus belts, clothing and homewares.

James Lock & Co
6 St James's Street, London SW1A 1EF
(men's 020 7930 8874/women's 020
7930 2421/www.lockhatters.co.uk)
London's oldest hatters, established in the 17th century.

Lulu Guinness
3 Ellis Street, London SW1X 9AL (020
7823 4828/www.luluguinness.com)
As well as the decorative, look-at-me bags designed to resemble fans, buckets of roses or birdcages, the range now includes shoes, compacts, perfume and other accessories.

Ollie & Nic
5 St Christopher's Place, London
W1U 1NA (020 7935 2160/
www.ollieandnic.com)
Inexpensive, brightly patterned handbags and accessories.

Osprey
11 St Christopher's Place, London
W1U 1NG (020 7935 2824/
www.ospreylondon.com)
Good quality yet affordable classic handbags.

Philip Treacy
69 Elizabeth Street, London SW1W 9PJ
(020 7730 3992/www.philiptreacy.co.uk)
London's top milliner is known for his

spectacular catwalk confections, but there is also a more casual ready-to-wear line.

Swaine Adeney Brigg
54 St James's Street, London SW1A 1JT
(020 7409 7277/www.swaineadeney.co.uk)
Hand-crafted umbrellas, luggage and briefcases, traditional riding accessories and other sporting and countryside requisites.

Tanner Krolle
3 Burlington Gardens, London W1S 3EW
(020 7287 5121/www.tannerkrolle.co.uk)
Contemporary and classic bags and holdalls.

JEWELLERY
Angela Hale
5 Royal Arcade, 28 Old Bond Street, London W1S 4SE (020 7495 1920/
www.angela-hale.co.uk)
Handmade costume jewellery drawing on Edwardian styles.

Boodles
1 Sloane Street, London SW1X 9LA
(020 7235 0111/www.boodles.com)
Long-established classic jewellers.

Cartier
175-176 New Bond Street, London W1S 4RN (020 7408 5700/www.cartier.com)
One of the best known names for watches and jewellery.

Dinny Hall
200 Westbourne Grove, London W11 2RH
(020 7792 3913/www.dinnyhall.com)
Minimalist, modern designs, such as single-drop pendants.

Erickson Beamon
38 Elizabeth Street, London SW1W 9NZ
(020 7259 0202/
www.ericksonbeamon.com)
Dramatic, often ethnic-inspired jewellery is the dominant look at this well-known design partnership.

Ernest Jones
277 Oxford Street, London W1C 2BR
(020 7629 6581/www.ernestjones.co.uk)
A destination for new and exclusive branded watches, exceptional service and a broad range of breathtaking diamond and jewellery collections.

Folli Follie
120 New Bond Street, London W1S 1EW
(0207 499 6633/www.folli-follie.co.uk)
Fantastic and out of the ordinary modern jewellery in gold and silver, luxury handbags with the sexiest collection of accessories and watches.

Fred
174 New Bond Street, London W1S 4RG
(020 7495 6303/www.fred.com)
French jewellery house with styles from modern minimalist to colourful and flamboyant.

Garrard
24 Albemarle Street, London W1S 4HT
(020 7758 8520/www.garrard.com)
The crown jeweller has been brought bang up to date by creative director Jade Jagger, with contemporary collections featuring diamonds and other precious gems.

Georg Jensen
15 New Bond Street, London W1S 3ST
(020 7499 6541/www.georgjensen.com)
Danish design house, established 1904, known for simplicity and modernity.

Harry Winston
171 New Bond Street, London W1S 4RD
(020 7907 8800/www.harrywinston.com)
Harry Winston is widely recognised as the King of Diamonds. After the much-awaited opening of their London flagship on Bond Street last year, Harry Winston has become just about the most glamorous way to buy diamonds and jewellery in the capital. A must for connoisseurs.

H Samuel
250 Oxford Street, London W1C 2DJ
(0207 493 1682/www.hsamuel.co.uk)
Britain's most popular jewellery store offering the widest range of great value classic and fashion pieces, branded watches and exemplary service.

Jess James
3 Newburgh Street, London W1F 7RE
(020 7437 0199/www.jessjames.com)
Long-standing champion of young, contemporary designers, the shop also has its own-label wedding and engagement rings and a selection of watches.

Kabiri
37 Marylebone High Street, London W1U 4QE (020 7224 1808/www.kabiri.co.uk)
An array of interesting modern jewellery from around 100 globe-spanning designers.

Lesley Craze Gallery
33-35A Clerkenwell Green, London EC1R 0DU (020 7608 0393/
www.lesleycrazegallery.co.uk)
Handmade jewellery and textiles from an international stable of designers.

Links of London
24 Lime Street, London EC3M 7HF
(020 7623 3101/www.linksoflondon.com)
Smart chain known for charm bracelets and sterling silver.

Tiffany & Co
25 Old Bond Street, London W1S 4QB
(020 7409 2790/www.tiffany.com/uk)
One of the world's most famous jewelers, specialises in diamonds and sculptural gold and silver pendants and charm bracelets.

Theo Fennell
169 Fulham Road, London SW3 6SP
(020 7591 5000/www.theofennell.com)
Statement jewellery and a nice line in sterling silver accessories including Marmite lids and tabasco bottle holders.

Wint &Kidd
237 Westbourne Grove, London W11 2SE
(020 7908 9990/www.wintandkidd.com)
Contemporary diamonds.

Wright & Teague
1A Grafton Street, London W1S 4EB (020 7629 2777/www.wrightandteague.com)
Known for boho-chic necklaces and bracelets with clusters of charms.

SALES AND DISCOUNT OUTLETS
Browns Labels for Less
50 South Molton Street, London W1K 5RD
(020 7514 0052/www.brownsfashion.com)
Previous seasons' collections from Browns boutique at 30-90 per cent off.

Burberry Factory Shop
29-53 Chatham Place, London E9 6LP
(020 8328 4287)
A vast warehouse full of seconds and excess stock - clothes for men, women and children, plus accessories - at half price or less.

Designer Sale UK
Studio 95, Old Truman Brewery, 95A Brick Lane, London E1 6QL (mailing list 01273 470880/during sale week 020 7247 8595/www.designersales.co.uk)
Held several times a year, stock from over 70 designers such as Alexander McQueen, Stella McCartney and Orla Kiely reduced by 40-90 per cent.

Designer Warehouse Sales
45 Balfe Street, London N1 9EF (020 7837 3322/www.designerwarehousesales.com)
DWS holds the only dedicated designer menswear sales in London, as well as separate womenswear sales, throughout the year. There's also a Nicole Farhi sale twice a year and a Ghost sale in the summer.

Paul Smith Sale Shop
23 Avery Row, London W1X 9HB
(020 7493 1287/www.paulsmith.co.uk)
Stock from previous seasons at up to 50 per cent off.

Index

A Bathing Ape 40
Action Man 35
Arcadia 20
Armani 44
Armani, Giorgio 57
Asda 14

Bag Hag, The 38
bags 38, 95, 137, *139*, 138
Bargainista, The 44
Ben Sherman 45
Biba 171
Bicester Village 22
Birmingham 23
Blacks 35
Bloomingdale's 95
Bluewater 22
Bonwit Teller 61
Brent Cross 22

Carhartt 40
carrier bags 95
Chanel 49
Chatty Cathy 72
Christmas 58, 100, 109, 111
Classicist, The 31
coats 126, 127
Comfort & Joy 171-2
Comme des Garçons 34
complaining
    court, going to 152
    diplomacy and 150
    letters 151-2
    to management 152
    rights, knowing your 154-5
counterfeits 163-4
credit cards 158
Crew 43
cruise lines 102

Dali, Salvador 61
Dapper David 41
Debenhams 20, 46
'demand items' 86, 87
deposits 159
designer clothes 79, 102, 106
Diana's Shop 33
discounts 108
Dolce & Gabbana 48
Don't-know Darren 73
dresses 128, 129
dressing for shopping 117
dry cleaning 157
Duffer 40

Eager Eva 71
eBay 44
ethical clothing 16
Farah 43
fashion shows 101, 102, 106, 108
Fashionista, The 34

flea market 36
Forever Forty, The 33
French Connection 62

Gap 33, 46
Gucci 48

Hackett 43
Handmade and Found 171-4, *172*
Harvey Nichols 23, 38, 48, 62, 174
haste, buying in 119
haute couture 101
Helly Hansen 35
Hermes 49
high street 20
Homeboy 178, *179*
Hugo Boss 41
Hulanicki, Barbara 171

independent shops 25, 68, 173
internet shopping 17
    auctions 165
    fraud 165
    going online before you shop 119
    percentage of women shopping
        through 17
    your rights 165, 167

Jack Wilson 43
Jacques Vert 31
Jaeger 32
jeans 123, *125*, 124
jewellery 140, 141
John Lewis 31
Johns, Jasper 59
Joseph 31
Ju Ju 180, 181, *181*

Kinigstein, Joseph 95

La Rinascente 57 175
Label Lover, The 48
layout of store/shop 173, 175-6
back of store 87
    buzzer entry systems 172
    carrier bags 95
colour 59, 64
    decompression zone 85
    demand items 86, 87
    destination area 87
    door 85
    fitting rooms 93-4, 173
    hot spots 80, 86
    interest levels and 86
lighting 65, 90, 94, 173
    music 93
    must haves 87
        racks 79, *82*
    sight lines 86
    signs 92
    smells 91

strike zone 86
    till 87
    windows 56-65, 174, 177
Lazarris, Diana 175, 176, *176*, 177
Leeds 23
lingerie 120, *121*, 122
Llewellyn, Ruth 171-2, 173, 174
London 19
    Bond Street 19, 38
    Brent Cross 22
    Camden Market 18
    catwalk shows 108
    Dover Street Market 48
    Essex Road 171
    Goldbourne Road 34
    Kensington High Street 171
    King's Road 19
    Notting Hill 19
    Oxford Circus 76
    Oxford Street 19
    Portobello Road 18, 19
    Saville Row 19
Louis Vuitton 48

malls 22
Manchester 23
mannequins 64, 65
markets, street 19
Marks & Spencer 19, 20
Martin Margiela 34
Massimo Dutti 39
Matalan 14, 40
Maxmara 31
Milan 19, 101, 102, 106, 108
Millets 35
Miss Vintage 36
money, how shops make more 83
Mr and Mrs Safe 46
'must haves' 87

Nerd, The 38
New Look 14, 20
New York 103, 108, 111
Next 20, 45
Nicole Farhi 31, 177
Nike Town 19
North Face 35

Oasis 37
One One Seven 175, 176, *176*, 177
Originator, The 49
Oxfam 37

Paris 19, 101, 102, 106, 109
Patagonia 35
pavement power 62
payment methods 158-61
Pop Art 59
Posh Girl, The 43
Prada 40, 48
prices 79, 83, 173

---

index/with thanks

Primark 19, 20, 40
private sales 164
privilege lists 106
promotions 83

Ralph Lauren 43
Rauschenberg, Robert 59
Reiss 41, 45
Rellik 37
Retro 34
Rohan 35
Rosenquist, James 59

sales 100, 102, 106, 108, 109, 111
Saturday Nighter, The 45
saturday, shopping on a 117
Seen 178-9, *179*
Selfridges 19, 23, 34, 38, 48
selling tribes 70-4
service and staff 66-9, 77, 117
    closing the sale 69
    independents 173
    training 66, 68
    turnover 68
shoes 133, *134*, 135, 136

shop stories 171-81
shopability 76-83
shopping times, average 88, 89
shopping tribes 30-49
Spot-on Suzy 74
store cards 106, 161

tailoring, men's 130, *131*, 132
Taylor, Jock 178, 179, *179*
Taylor, Keith 178, 179, *179*
Tesco 14
Thomas Pink 41
TK Maxx 14, 44
Tods 31
Top Shop 37, 76

Valentines Day 58
value 14
VIC (very important customers) 106
vintage clothing 18, 36-7

warehouse sales 102, 106, 108
Warhol, Andy 59
watches 19, 142, 143
Watches of Switzerland 19

when to shop 98, 99
    January 100-1
    February 102
    March 105
    April/May 105
    June/July 106
    August 108
    September 108
    October/November 109
    December 111
Wilson, Anthony 171, 173, 174
windows 56-65, 177
    as advertising space 56
    budgets for 56
    colour 59
    concept 57
    crimes 58
    dressers 57, 58, 59, 61, 174
    how to read a 64-5
    pavement power 62

YSL 45

Zara 41, 62
Zegna 41

WITH THANKS
A huge thank you to the team at BBC Books. To the passionate Shirley Patton who was the first to share the vision! To the exacting Eleanor Maxfield and Gillian Haslam who kept us on track. To Hannah Telfer, Diana, Vincent, Salma, Alex and Claire who made it all happen. Thanks, also, to the team at Smith & Gilmour for their passion and beautiful design work.

To the team at Optomen Television, quite simply the most brilliant team of people on the telly who have come with me fearlessly into some of the scariest shops in the country and given them back their passion and hope in what is an increasingly competitive climate. To Executive Producer Pat Llewellyn who believed in me right from the start and the visionary Ben Adler. To the passionate, talented and hard-working series producer Becky Clarke who pulled it all together, even in our darkest moments, and her team of directors, the majestic Martha, beautiful Diene, sleepless David and gorgeous Jenny. Thanks to Anna, for trying to make me look beautiful, and to Rex, the soundman, for constantly putting his hand down my shirt. Thanks also to Emily, Kym and Stephen and a special thank you to Faye Donaldson (aka Olive) – a star in the making – and the grumpy, cute and brilliant cameraman Richard.

In appreciation of my team and colleagues at Yellowdoor, the most creative and fearless retail communications agency in London. To my business partner Peter Cross who embarked on this journey with me and is still there. And a special thank you to my team of directors at Yellowdoor who have all played their part and my tireless PA Ariana, who has made sure that I've always packed my clean knickers.

To the wonderfully talented Josh Sims who has consistently and creatively delivered beyond the call of duty.

To Iain Renwick and William Matthews at Liberty, my favourite shop in the world. And Harvey Nichols, a special shop to me personally. For their help with the research, thanks to Clarks, Gossard, Fullcircle, Ernest Jones, Topshop, Louis Vuitton, Matches, Hannah Russell at Oasis, Vivienne Becker and Ben Cobb. With thanks to the following companies whose amazing products have helped make this book look so brilliant: Bailey of Hollywood, Clarks, Clarks Originals, Comptoir des Cotonniers, Crew Clothing Co., Crew Clothing Childrenswear, dunhill, Ernest Jones, Folli Follie, French Connection, Fullcircle, Fullcircle Footwear, Gossard, H Samuel, Harry Winston, Helen Green Design, Holland & Holland, Homebase, Jacques Vert, John Smedley, Jesiré, Oasis, Planet, Precis Petite, Ronit Zilkha, Somi, Sportsgirl, Stuart Weitzman, Sussan and Windsmoor. And to Andrew Meredith and Selfridges for their contribution of stunning shop window images.

And finally a special thank you to my family. For letting me stay away overnight, come home late, miss the holidays and school runs, forget to pack the lunches and generally not be a supermum to make sure this book gets to print on time.

Author's note
To all the many retailers and sources of information who have been quoted in this book: while I have made every effort to credit those responsible for the work, any such omissions are greatly regretted – my sincere apologies. Mary Portas can be contacted directly at mary@maryqueenofshops.com